DEDICATION

Dedicated to the loving memory of:

Laura and Archiebald Chapman

Ora Knight and William Dixie Tiller

Dean Dwight Crisp

Acknowledgement

Many of the basic concepts and ideas in this publication came from Sister Patricia Murphy O.L.V., a nationally recognized authority on family issues related to senior members. Only through discussions and critical reviews by Sister Murphy did the manuscript finally take its focus. Although her expertise helped in the formation of several chapters, it was especially appreciated (and perhaps most noticeable) in the answers to the Family Case Studies. I hope this practical, self-paced book accurately reflects Sister Murphy's professionalism. Her contributions are greatly appreciated.

Elwood N. Chapman

The Unfinished Business Of Living

Helping Aging Parents Help Themselves

ELWOOD N. CHAPMAN

Crisp Publications, Inc.
Los Altos, California

The Unfinished Business Of Living
Helping Aging Parents Help Themselves

by Elwood N. Chapman

Crisp Publications, Inc.
95 First Street
Los Altos, CA 94022

Library of Congress Catalog Card Number 86-71572

Chapman, Elwood N.

ISBN 0-931961-19-X

Printed in the United States of America.

Cover design by Carol Harris.

Preface

This book is directed to those in the middle generation who must deal with their children on one hand, and their aging parents on the other. The central theme of *The Unfinished Business Of Living* rests on the premise that when senior family members receive reasonable and sensitive support, all other members, regardless of age, benefit.

Following are some goals that readers of this book might strive for:

- Greater awareness of recognizing and adapting to diminishing capabilities of senior family members.

- Greater skill in dealing with decisions involving the well-being of the elderly.

- Commitment to building a family support strategy.

- Reduced pressure so adult children can enjoy their parents more.

- Minimized guilt among family members.

- A greater insight into the aging process.

The author recognizes that relationships within your family circle are your private domain. Although The *Unfinished Business of Living* provides guidance and direction, you must accept or reject specific suggestions based on your own family situation and what is comfortable for you. I wrote this book both as a guide to be read now, and used as a reference later when problems surface. The book is ideal to circulate within a family circle.

At the end of each chapter are two *family studies*. These are designed to encourage individual thinking. Although only a few may relate directly to your personal situation, you are encouraged to read and discuss them all.

"There are only two lasting bequests

we can hope to give our children.

One of these is roots: the other wings."

Hodding Carter

Contents

Traveling by automobile through Tucumcari, New Mexico, I picked up a discarded local newspaper while having breakfast in a small cafe. The following notice was given a choice location:

Edgar Sparks

will celebrate his

90th Birthday

on

August 28, 1983.

Friends and neighbors are invited to stop by for cake and refreshments at the

Portales Inn from 2:00 — 4:30 p.m.

He thinks there's a chance he might not make it to a hundred and had rather have a big birthday celebration than a big funeral. *Y'all Come.*

My wife and I were tempted to stay over and attend the party because we would have enjoyed meeting Edgar and his wonderful friends who thought enough of him to arrange the celebration and put the announcement in the paper. We hope everyone had a great time, especially Edgar.

A Special Challenge From The Author

A few years ago I participated in a role-playing experience designed to help me better understand what it is like to be much older (I am currently age 70). My eyesight was impaired by a pair of dark goggles, cotton was inserted in my ears, one leg was hobbled, and I was given a canc and ushered into a hotel lobby to meet strangers. The experiment worked. I came away with a new insight I would like to share.

From the perspective of an aging individual, the positive side of unfinished business is finding personal fulfillment—a time to convert one's last years into new beauty and spiritual growth. The negative side of unfinished business are the frustrations of coping with the handicaps of the aging process. Often fulfillment can play second fiddle to "just surviving."

Fulfillment among those fortunate enough to extend their lives into later years can take many forms. For a few individuals it is a final creative splurge; for others it can be a successful effort to bring a family closer together; for still others fulfillment can be a new spiritual awareness. Some reach inner-satisfaction through better understanding of what their lives have been about and write their memoirs. Some may take an overdue "dream trip." The possibilities are endless and exciting. These are the positive aspects of unfinished business.

In one sense, the final phase of living should be the most fulfilling of all. There should be laughter. There should be "happy times." There should be a degree of peace and understanding.

After all, happiness should be the basic goal of retirement. Without some degree of fulfillment to look forward to, why struggle through the last phase of life? Why even deal with unfinished business?

Those who reach a satisfactory level of happiness late in life often pay a high price because the challenges are greater than in earlier years. Each "happy time" is accomplished despite problems that come with aging. Small wonder that the lives of many elderly seem to be 95% survival and 5% fulfillment. Yet, despite these odds, most individuals can achieve a balance between the two sides of unfinished business. They earn the satisfaction that comes from knowing they have finished their lives with beauty and style...and that much of it, they did alone.

Claire is 85 and a widow of twelve years. She has all the frustrations of dealing with the survival aspects of living. Claire has constant pain from arthritis. Despite this, she finds fulfillment through gardening, painting, and visits from her family and friends. Claire is the first to admit that she needs a little help along the way: "It is tough going it alone in my own home at my age, but a little daily happiness because someone pays me a visit, or brings me a special treat, makes it all worthwhile."

Jake is 82 and proud that he is doing really well. Getting through a day is about all he can handle. When asked how he was doing a few years ago he replied, "I'm existing." Today, he would answer differently because a few months ago his family got together and started to build some support for Jake. Now, he has a twice-a-week housekeeper, family visitations on a regular basis, and hot meals delivered to his door. Not a lot, but enough for Jake to become much more positive and enjoy some of the simple pleasures. Jake is writing his memoirs and sharing the project with family members.

Both Claire and Jake's family should be congratulated for recognizing a little help goes a long way.

As you read *The Unfinished Business of Living*, remind yourself that without some fulfillment, an older person may find the last phase of life very empty. With just a little effort by a family member, however, a more beautiful side of finishing unfinished business can take place.

Elwood N. Chapman

Aging In America—
A Self Test

How much do you know about aging in America and the intergenerational challenges of the future? Listed below are 20 statements that will help prepare you for the chapters ahead. You are invited to agree or disagree with each statement and then compare your answers with those of the author.

Agree	Disagree	
_____	_____	1. If you are caught between the responsibilities of raising children and caring for aging parents, you are a member of the "sandwich generation."
_____	_____	2. Adult children today show less concern for their parents than in the past.
_____	_____	3. Generally speaking, once someone has retired, family relationships become increasingly important.
_____	_____	4. Because of technological advances in medicine, chances are good that you will reach an older age than your parents.
_____	_____	5. Despite a variety of community care facilities for aging parents (once they cannot live alone), the primary option continues to be housing an aging parent in the home of a child.
_____	_____	6. The more encouragement to remain independent that an aging parent receives from family members, the longer institutional care can be postponed.
_____	_____	7. Almost 90% of unfinished business with aging parents takes care of itself.
_____	_____	8. Family members who assume care for highly fragile seniors can often become more depressed and angry than those they are trying to help.

_____ _____ 9. Young children who spend time with their grandparents benefit from receiving preliminary insights into the aging process.

_____ _____ 10. The less adult children learn about the aging process from their own parents, the better their own aging will be.

_____ _____ 11. Intergenerational sharing has become a lost art.

_____ _____ 12. Those who resist and/or deny family relationships often wind up dealing with the implications of their actions through the remainder of their lives.

_____ _____ 13. Positive reinforcement from family members is often available only during crisis periods.

_____ _____ 14. Families who learn to pull together on relationship issues tend to have better experiences when dealing with the financial aspects of unfinished business.

_____ _____ 15. In the United States during the past two decades, the over-65 population has grown at twice the rate of the rest of the population.

_____ _____ 16. Whatever you accomplish in a positive vein within your family circle helps to promote your individual development.

_____ _____ 17. Fifty percent of adult children live within an hour's drive of their parents.

_____ _____ 18. Many adult children provide needed support to their aging parents without being hands-on caregivers.

_____ _____ 19. Those who contribute most to their family circles gain the most in return.

_____ _____ 20. Family members who do their best to help aging parents, even though it may be far less than what other siblings contribute, should not foster guilt feelings within themselves.

MATCH YOUR RESPONSES: 1. Agree; 2. Disagree; 3. Agree; 4. Agree; 5. Agree; 6. Agree; 7. Disagree; 8. Agree; 9. Agree; 10. Disagree; 11. Disagree; 12. Agree; 13. Agree; 14. Agree; 15. Agree; 16. Agree; 17. Agree; 18. Agree; 19. Agree; 20. Agree.

What Is Meant By Unfinished Business

Unfinished business refers to all aspects involved in providing senior family members the support they need to complete their life cycle in dignity. To the senior it is a time to fulfill those promises made earlier in life, and still prepare things for successors. To the adult child it is a time when "Mom and Dad" can use some additional physical and emotional support. It is important to anticipate the unfinished business of living. Planning should begin early. Leaving too much business "unfinished" is damaging to seniors, adult children, and family unity.

The longer you live, the more unfinished business you will accumulate. Some of it is business-related (like doing a will, or shedding possessions). Mainly however, it is a time to repair and restore impaired relationships, or deal with truncated dreams.

Unfinished business is a family-team effort. The well-being of families, even after the death of parents, depends upon how well and how much of the accumulated unfinished business gets done. The fact that unfinished business is handed to future generations makes it even more important for both the senior and adult members of a family to take advantage of the grace period old age brings.

No one completely finishes the "business of living" during his or her lifetime. But the amount of attention invested in loving, forgiving, bequeathing and clarifying, makes all of the difference to the quality of life an older person and his or her family experiences.

1

You and Your Changing Family

"No matter how many communes anybody invents, the family always creeps back."
Margaret Mead

A family is the most intriguing, powerful, and self-serving of all social groups. Membership is often composed of a closely knit circle of individuals who share enriching experiences not easily duplicated in other social units. The most meaningful relationships we have are often found within our family. And most important of all, membership is seldom denied.

To most of us, a family provides identity, security, and stability. A family is where we receive our first lesson in interdependence. It is here that others help us face a bigger world. Families have a way of providing members of all ages with resources and assistance during emergencies. And at graduations, weddings, births, career promotions, and funerals, family support is often the music we most want to hear.

1

Yet, as important as families can be, recent changes threaten the role families may play in the future. When it comes to family circles, it is not business as usual.

NEW FAMILY CONFIGURATIONS

In the past, family circles were more compact geographically and closer emotionally. Life itself was simpler. Most individuals grew to maturity with the family farm or business as the "hub." Lines of communication were easier to maintain. Family gatherings and reunions were normal and frequent.

Today, however, family patterns are considerably more complex. Family members are increasingly mobile. As a result, maintaining a family focus is a greater challenge even though the benefits of family life are needed more than ever.

Three major trends are having significant impact upon family configurations. These are listed below. As you study them, think about your own family circle.

1. **Family members are living longer.**

   Medical advancements, improved diets, and other factors have extended our life span far beyond what it was only fifty years earlier.

   > Mr. and Mrs. Franks are over 60 years of age. Each has one parent still living. They also have three grown children, nine grandchildren, and two great-grandchildren. It is not unusual to have five generations present at a family gathering.

2. **Family circles are expanding due to an increased divorce rate.**

   > Mr. and Mrs. Grace are in their late forties. Their parents have just recently retired. Among their five children there have been seven grandchildren, three divorces and two remarriages. A new daughter-in-law brought four new children with her, causing the Grace family to grow dramatically.

3. Geographical dispersion is greater.

Modern families are often scattered so widely that it takes far greater effort and money to simply stay "in touch."

> Mr. and Mrs. James talk about their "international" family. With seven children (all mid-generation adults), they have grandchildren in four states and three foreign countries. Although 100% attendance at family gatherings is out of the question and face-to-face contact is infrequent, the monthly telephone bills indicate that considerable communication still takes place.

DIFFERENT KINDS OF FAMILIES

There are two basic kinds of family units. First is the nuclear (or primary) family, consisting of parents and their children living in one household. This is the typical traditional family unit —mother, father, and children. The second family unit is the extended family. This is a recent phrase developed to describe a group which may or may not live under one roof, but does gather frequently and sometimes functions as a family unit.

When you put nuclear and extended families together and then add a few intimate friends, you wind up with what is defined in this publication as a family circle. The size and composition of a family circle (or network) depends upon many factors. These can include the number of siblings from the original nuclear family; how many siblings marry and have nuclear families of their own; the number of divorces and remarriages that have occurred; plus any adoptions and/or intimate friends who have been invited into the circle.

YOUR OWN FAMILY CIRCLE

To help you gain a fresh focus on your own family, you are invited to complete the following exercise. Simply write the first name of appropriate individuals in each circle. Complete as much as you can in a few moments without including relatives such as cousins, nieces, or nephews (unless you have maintained close and meaningful relationships with them).

When finished, (1) place a star next to all names where the individual is over 70 years of age, and (2) place a circle next to those individuals who live more than 100 miles from you. Do not list those who are deceased.

YOUR FAMILY CIRCLE

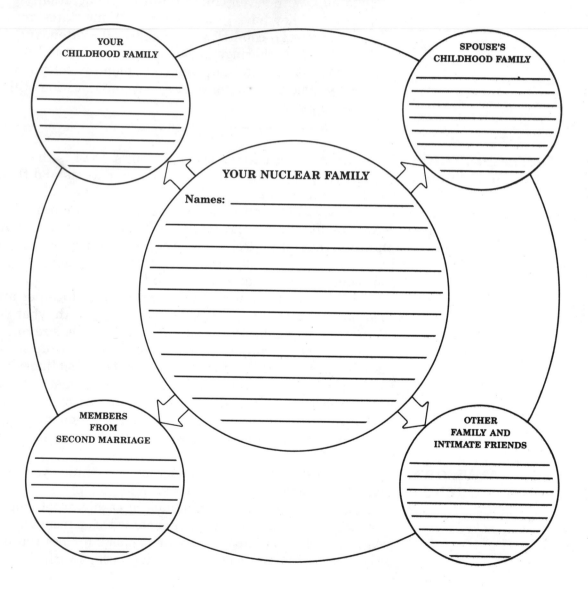

THE SIGNIFICANT ROLE OF SENIOR FAMILY MEMBERS

Inside a modern family circle, different generations continue to impact each other both vertically and horizontally. Values are often tested from many directions. In some families, growing older is respected and communication is free and open. In other family circles, senior members are kept at a distance. Two-way communication is lacking.

Although senior family members in the United States are not revered to the same degree as many other cultures, they usually are determined to stay involved. Some permit themselves to be pushed into passive or observation roles, while others fight to remain at "center stage." Regardless of the roles played, the existence of senior members is often a consciousness-raising challenge for the younger set. And no matter what attempts may be made to dismiss the matter, the process of aging within most families is increasingly present.

AGING PARENTS AND THE SEXUAL REVOLUTION

The "sexual revolution" has led to more working women, more divorces, and more single parents. It has also placed a premium on the amount of time many adult children can devote to aging parents. Increasing numbers of young people are so busy working, caring for children, and/or holding their lives together, their aging parents must often take care of themselves and/or depend more on community support programs.

Lynda's daily routine is common among many of her contemporaries. She is up early to get the children ready for school; commutes 30 minutes to a demanding job; returns home to chores and family needs including some communication with her busy husband. Although Lynda's aging mother could use frequent help, Lynda is lucky to see her once a month. Lynda told her best friend Gail: "I know it is not right and I feel guilty now and then, but with everything else on top of me, my mom, unfortunately, is a low priority."

As pressures on the "sandwich generation" increase, adult children, as well as senior family members, need to face reality and learn to work more closely with community support systems (chapter 8). This may provide a partial solution in the future. Adult children also need to learn new coping techniques to help them protect their own lives while learning to deal more effectively with aging parents.

A GREATER NEED FOR COPING MECHANISMS

Coping is the process of dealing with difficult problems without putting harmful pressure on your own emotional and mental health. A *mechanism* is a technique or approach that helps make successful coping possible. Coping mechanisms can be thought of as "safety valves" that permit a person to release their inner tensions harmlessly. An example of a healthy mechanism (safety valve) is sharing a problem openly with a friend or family member.

Some mechanisms are built-in. For example, shedding tears helps most people express and release their feelings. Some mechanisms, however, need to be *developed*. Properly developed mechanisms can prevent over-reacting to a situation, which can lead to improved understanding and forgiving.

A mentally healthy person is one who can deal effectively with problems without damaging self or relationships with others. One purpose of this book is to present some practical coping mechanisms for both adult children and aging parents so that unfinished business can be conducted calmly and relationships protected.

THE DOUBLE-DECKER SANDWICH GENERATION

The "sandwich generation" is involved in raising children on one side, and contributing to the well-being of aging parents on the other. Pressure comes from both sides and the "adult children" are caught in the middle.

There is also what we might call a double-decker (or double-whammy) sandwich generation. For example, it is increasingly possible for a person age 70 years to have concern about his or her 90 year-old parents, plus daily care of an ailing spouse, as well as concerns with adult children who are going through divorces or having financial problems. There may even be worries over the grandchildren. These unfortunate individuals have pressures from the older, their own, and two younger generations, and with less energy to cope than they once had.

What kind of support can be provided to help these special people? In most cases, additional support must come from younger family members, friends, neighbors, and/or community groups. Put another way, the care patterns and support systems suggested in *The Unfinished Business of Living* should be doubled. Even when extra personal support is impossible, at least the "double-whammy" aspects of the situation should be recognized by family members, and understanding should be transmitted by all concerned.

BETTER BALANCING IS THE CHALLENGE Most aging parents who would like or need more attention or assistance recognize that their children should give their grandchildren and spouses first priority. Some senior family members are sensitive to the fact that their adult children may be under more pressure than they were at the same stage in life. This does not mean, however, that they expect to be neglected or left out. Although many senior parents recognize it is time to leave center stage, most still want a significant role to play. A diminishing or minor role may be acceptable, but few wish to be relegated to non-participating backstage observers.

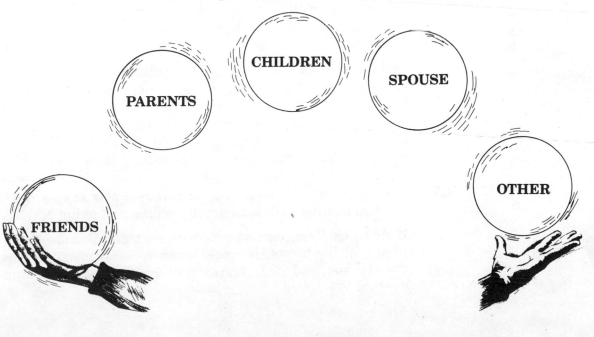

Senior family members need to be as self-reliant as their health permits. It is also a good idea to utilize non-family resources when available and appropriate. At the same time, mid-generation adults need to become more skillful at "balancing" the demands of their busy lives.

A primary goal of *The Unfinished Business of Living* is to assist adult children to learn how to juggle their many commitments without "dropping the ball" with their aging parents. This is not always an easy task! As a preview of ideas in this book, consider the following suggestions:

1. **Ask retired parents to help you.** This can include doing repairs in your home, babysitting, attending activities in your place, or taking care of selected business matters. These activities can make parents feel needed and relieve some of your pressures.

2. **If you have children, let them do some of the balancing for you.** Without overdoing it, the more you can arrange for your children to spend time with their grandparents, the better the relationships will be for all concerned.

3. **Do not allow your lifestyle to isolate you from parents.** If you are single and have a "live-in friend," try to bring this person into your family circle. Your parents can probably handle this situation better than you suspect.

As you proceed with your private balancing act, keep in mind that even the best juggler will drop a ball now and then. Whenever this happens with your parents, try to restore the relationship as soon as possible. Of all the relationships you may be juggling, your parents will probably forgive and forget more gracefully than others.

SUMMARY
(1) Changes within family circles mandate new approaches when dealing with both adult children and aging parents.

(2) Adult children need more assistance today because their parents live longer, distances between family members may be greater, and life is increasingly complex and demanding.

(3) Material presented in this book is a challenge and an opportunity for both adult children *and* their aging parents. Those who accept the challenge can enhance their own lives while improving family ties.

AUTHOR'S NOTE:

At the end of each chapter in this book you will find two family studies. Each is designed to involve you in a reality-based situation that deals with the unfinished business of a senior family member. Although these studies are excellent for group discussions; they are also self-instructional. In either situation, the reader is encouraged to study each case, write an answer, discuss it with another party (especially a spouse), and then compare conclusions reached with those of the author at the end of the book.

FAMILY STUDY #1　　**Jerome's Dilemma**

Jerome is the only son and youngest sibling in the Henderson family. He and his large nuclear family live in California. Jerome's mother and father live in Oklahoma, near his three sisters. The eldest sister, Lois, has remained single and assumed major leadership as far as watching out for the "folks."

Jerome's mother has called him three times during the past week to discuss his father who recently had two minor accidents while driving. Mr. Henderson barely passed the vision part of his driving examination and, as a result, received only a one year extension to his license. Jerome's father will be 86 on his next birthday, and has a strong, independent nature. In the eyes of the rest of the family, including Lois, Jerome is the only one who can influence or deal with his father.

Jerome, concerned about the anxiety in his mother's voice, considers these options:

1. Call Lois and get the lowdown.

2. Call his dad and get his dad's view on what is going on.

3. Call Lois and ask her to discuss the matter with the family doctor for additional data on their father's general health and failing eyesight. Ask her to share what she discovers with him and their two sisters.

4. Do nothing and trust to luck that his father will eventually make the decision on his own to give up driving.

5. Fly to Oklahoma to discuss the matter directly with his father.

6. Do nothing until his parents' golden wedding anniversary next year. Pacify his mother until them.

Which of the above would you recommend? In which order? Write them down in the spaces provided with other suggestions you would make and then compare with those found on page 199.

_____

_____

_____

_____

_____

_____

_____

FAMILY STUDY #2   **Sylvia Blows Her Top**

Nobody expected it, but Sylvia—the youngest of six
children—disrupted a recent family meeting with some
powerful comments. Here is what happened:

The sibling "get-together" was called to plan a 50th
wedding celebration for their parents. During the discussion,
everyone but Sylvia seemed to agree that the folks would
need more support in the future and less should be
expected from them. The single comment that caused the
overreaction from Sylvia was her older brother saying,
"They have made their contribution and deserve the
opportunity to sit back and observe." This caused Sylvia to
say, "I have this strange feeling you are underestimating
our parents. They are still active people. They are only 75
and their creative powers are as alive as ever. What we
need to do is find ways to continue their involvement. The
attitude I hear is, let's put the folks on a shelf. Perhaps for
your own convenience, you are writing them off too soon.
The truth is that you are not old anymore at age 75. We are
planning a celebration, not a wake."

Do you agree or disagree with Sylvia? Write your comments
below and then read the comments on page 199.

_____

_____

_____

_____

_____

_____

2

Support Is Better
When It Is A Family Affair

"It's kinder funny, but no matter how common our blood is, we hate to lose any of it."
Will Rogers

It is always encouraging to hear that a single family member has stepped forward to monitor and supervise the care of an aging parent. This often happens when:

• One sibling lives closer than others.

• One family member has enjoyed a closer relationship.

• One sibling has a more understanding spouse.

• One nuclear family member decides that having Mom or Dad come to live with them would be beneficial to all.

• There is only one child.

13

Although such action is to be admired, whenever possible care of senior members should involve all family members. There are two basic reasons why this is true. First, involvements can be shared more evenly to avoid a strain on any individual. Second, the aging parent will enjoy the attention, support, and love from a cohesive, undivided family. This, in many situations, is a lifelong goal for senior family members.

Whether any family can operate as a team to provide the best possible support system depends on many factors, including the following four practical considerations that deserve attention: (1) Is there enough open communication within the family to arrive at good group decisions? (2) Are there family members who can provide sensitive leadership on a temporary basis? (3) Are members willing to get together when required to "make the major decisions?" (4) Is there sufficient sensitivity to know when to intervene and when to give parents the right to live what we might consider somewhat imperfect lives?

IT ALL STARTS WITH OPEN COMMUNICATION

It may sound ridiculously simple, but families who talk with each other have a giant edge over families that don't. When there is open communication, families are less apt to act on their own. When family members are excluded from any situation (good or bad), resentments can quickly build. This is true when members have not made attempts to "keep in touch." For example, if one well-meaning family member encourages a senior parent to make a minor decision (like selling a possession or taking a trip) without communicating with others in the family, relationships can be damaged and decisions in the future may be more difficult to reach.

Communication is necessary when a minor decision is to be made. *When the health and future of an aging parent is involved, communication within a family circle is critical.* Consider the following advantages to family (shared) decision making.

(1) Those involved in the process may start giving more support to the aging parent. Simply being involved has a way of making participants out of observers.

(2) Shared decisions are less intrusive because everyone has a chance to protect their turf ahead of time. The term "meddler" is less apt to surface.

(3) An ultimate intervention is more apt to be in the best interests of member(s) and family as a whole, because when all aspects are discussed ahead of time, fewer unanticipated and/or dangerous side effects develop.

(4) Families that learn how to make group decisions during beginning phases of "unfinished business" are better prepared to make crisis decisions later.

(5) Nothing seems to please aging parents more than to sense that their family is working as a team to help them make the best decisions.

OBSTACLES TO FAMILY PROBLEM SOLVING

When it comes to logical problem solving, the handicaps family circles may face can be so great that, despite open communication, reasonable solutions may be out of reach. Consider these roadblocks.

- **Secrecy Tendencies.** A few family circles have secrets so pervasive that solving a family problem is like playing poker with a short deck. Hidden motives (a form of secrecy) cloud the decision-making process to the point that *any* decision is welcome, just to get the process over with quickly.

- **Suppressed Feelings.** Too often in family discussions , one or more member continues to wear childhood emotions on his or her sleeve. When such matters surface, the decision-making process is often distorted or aborted because irrational, pent-up emotions are released.

Although the above obstacles may appear too formidable to overcome, this is not always the case. More often than not a crisis situation centered around "grandma" or "grandpa" helps restore family relationships — sometimes on a permanent basis. Of course, those families who concentrate on communication in advance have a big advantage over those who don't.

The exercise that follows may suggest some improvements you should consider now, in order to prepare for the future.

COMMUNICATION ENHANCEMENT EXERCISE

Communication within any family configuration can be divided into two classifications — face-to-face conversations and alternatives. Nothing can take the place of intimate communication that occurs during personal visits or family gatherings. These should be treated as "special moments" and all conversational skills (listening, complimenting, laughing) should be employed. However, due to the increased geographical dispersion of family members, alternatives are increasingly important. Modern technology provides us with many ways to enhance communication from a distance. From the communication enhancements listed below, check three that you feel you can make better use of.

TELEPHONE

☐

In addition to special "frequent caller" rates in some areas, it is now possible to arrange for three-way family conversations through regular residential telephones. (Call your local telephone company for details.) The biggest barrier to greater telephone use in some families is the cost, especially among senior members who have not been able to adjust to higher rates.

> Jack has been paying his mother's telephone bill for years so she can call any family member at any time without worrying about the cost. She is careful to call long distance during off hours, but when she needs to call, she doesn't hesitate. Jack does not discuss the amount of each bill with his mother, assuming she would prefer not to know.

COMMUNICATION ENHANCEMENT EXERCISE (cont.)

**LETTERS/CARD
ROUND ROBINS**

☐

Although some family members are far better at using the mail service than others, the advantages, especially to senior members, are many. A letter, card, or round robin (a letter that goes from one person to another within a family where each person can add to the initial message) can be read, reread and shared with others. A few turn into family treasures.

> Mrs. King, a widow at 62, keeps a file on the birthdays and anniversaries of family members and sends everyone gifts to celebrate these occasions. When grandchildren and great grandchildren are involved, the gift is often a cute card with a few dollars added. Best of all, she shares the process with her 92 year old mother, who lives with her.

**PHOTOGRAPHS/
ARTWORK**

☐

A picture of an adult may not be worth a thousand words, but a picture of a grandchild to a grandparent may be worth more. One might need to use caution in sending pictures to other family members, but never grandparents.

> Mary has kept her parents close to her three children by keeping them informed on their activities and sending pictures frequently. Along with each photograph, she usually sends some artwork done by the children. It is a great combination.

COMMUNICATION ENHANCEMENT EXERCISE (cont.)

**AUDIO/
VIDEO TAPES**

☐

More and more families are keeping in touch through the use of audio tapes and video cassettes.

> Every few months Joe makes a video cassette featuring the children and sends it to both his parents and his wife's mother. It is the next best thing to being there.

BULLETINS

☐

The larger a family and the more geographically dispersed it becomes, the more effective a printed or duplicated bulletin can be.

> Sally is known as the information magnet of her family circle (five nuclear units) and enjoys preparing and mailing a bulletin every now and them. Sally gets other members to make contributions, but uses her creativity and humor to put it all together. Isolated in Florida with a limited travel budget, it makes her feel better to provide this much-appreciated family service.

FAMILY
LEADERSHIP

Family leadership roles are often vastly different than those found in business and community activities. One reason is that leadership is often assumed due to special circumstances. For example, a sibling who lives geographically close to an aging parent while others have moved away, often accepts "leadership by proximity." Also, leadership is sometimes centered around a crisis situation relating to aging parents and thus is temporary in nature; once a decision has been made, the leadership role is often relinquished. Finally, within a family, the traditional "leader-follower" pattern is not fully applicable. For example, one family member could be a leader in helping a parent solve a home safety problem but a follower on financial matters. Leadership roles are often passed around or rotated within a family circle. In all situations, however, the aging parent should be involved.

None of this should be interpreted to mean that family leadership is less challenging than in a business situation. Not so! To play even a temporary leadership role requires great sensitivity and understanding.

You are invited to assess your own family leadership potential in the exercise that follows. As you do this, keep in mind that successful business or community leaders do not necessarily make good family leaders; and conversely, followers in other environments can make excellent family leaders.

FAMILY LEADERSHIP EXERCISE

Place a ☑ opposite those characteristics you have already demonstrated within your family circle; then go over the list a second time and place an ⊠ opposite those that you would be willing to demonstate in the future.

☐ Setting a leadership example by providing the best possible personal support to aging parents.

☐ Spending time keeping family members informed on the condition of aging parents.

☐ Acting as a general information magnet to keep everyone within the family circle informed on all important family matters.

☐ Recognizing and demonstrating that a family leadership role is a *giving role* and not one of authority.

☐ Using a "group process" to gain the acceptance of a decision from key family members.

☐ Leading in such a sensitive manner that old resentments are not activated and new ones are not created.

☐ Being a "positive force" within the family during both calm and crisis periods.

☐ Showing your leadership by supporting the family member living closest to aging parents.

☐ Sensing when there is a "leadership void" and volunteering when needed.

☐ Working to rotate leadership roles according to what each family member can do best.

☐ Giving full recognition to leadership contributions made by others and not feeling resentful when you may not receive full recognition for your own leadership roles.

☐ Being knowledgeable about community supports and using them appropriately.

☐ Showing tolerance to the leadership efforts of others, i.e., being a good follower.

SERIOUS FAMILY MEETINGS

A family gathering to solve a serious problem involving an aging parent can be initiated by:

- The senior family member

- A family member

- A doctor

- A minister

- A social worker

- A friend

Support from friends, neighbors, local religious leaders, social workers, family counselors, and health professionals should be accepted and sought by family members. Sometimes these professionals should be present at family meetings. Families, however, should not back away from providing all possible support themselves.

With this in mind, assume that you are willing to initiate and play a temporary leadership role to provide family support for an older person you dearly love. Further, assume that your family (as presently constructed) has never come together to make a major decision concerning a senior family menber. To prepare for the meeting, you decide to complete the following exercise.

"POW-WOW" EXERCISE

Under the best circumstances, the decision-making process can be difficult, so once the need for a family conference has been established, setting a date and location should take time schedules, travel distances, and other factors of all family members into consideration. In the vast majority of cases, the location should be where the senior member(s) reside. Once assembled, the following suggestions are submitted. Indicate whether you agree or disagree.

Agree   *Disagree*

_____   _____   1. If senior family members are present and capable, encourage them to conduct the meeting. If this is impossible, do the next best thing, ensure they become involved. Their input is vital to how they accept the final decision.

_____   _____   2. In conducting the meeting, keep the climate of the meeting serious until each person has had a chance to fully express his or her opinion. Welcome all suggestions.

_____   _____   3. If one family member is hesitant to make a contribution or is visually showing some hostility, ask for their views.

_____   _____   4. If a family member was unable to attend but has submitted their views in writing, read that communication early in the meeting; if the member has appointed another to speak for him or her (health data, living options, financial considerations), sufficient time should be provided for data to be presented.

_____   _____   5. Any research should be submitted to the group early in the meeting by the person who conducted the investigation.

"POW-WOW" EXERCISE (cont.)

Agree   *Disagree*

_____   _____   6. The person conducting the meeting should keep in mind that the communication taking place between family members may be almost as important as the decision itself. A quick decision should not be forced.

_____   _____   7. For good decision making, the options available should be reduced to three or less whenever possible.

_____   _____   8. The final goal is unanimous acceptance of the majority, but an infantile or selfish reason should not hold up an important and necessary intervention.

_____   _____   9. Have confidence in your style while conducting the meeting. The more relaxed and informal, the better.

_____   _____   10. Include any senior member(s) present and seek his or her reaction to comments made.

_____   _____   11. Once a decision has been reached, family volunteers may be requested to implement it. This is especially true when financial support is necessary. Time should be taken to accomplish this.

_____   _____   12. Once the serious part of the meeting is over (as short as possible to accomplish goals), the "good times" should start.

SPECIAL NOTE: THERE MAY BE REASONS WHY A FAMILY MEETING IS NOT A GOOD IDEA. Three examples include: (1) if controversy within the family circle is such that a meeting might open up an unrelated "can of worms"; (2) if such a meeting would have a highly detrimental influence on the physical or emotional health of the senior family member that the meeting is designed to help; (3) if conducting such a meeting would affect your own mental or physical health.

Sharing the pressure and responsibility for the care of an aging parent among family members is a sensitive undertaking. Small wonder that now and then one child may throw up his or her hands and assume the major responsibility. As tempting as this may be at times, it should be avoided. A senior family member belongs to the entire family. Equal participation may be asking too much, but where possible, everyone should be given the opportunity to become involved and contribute. It is this approach that will strengthen the family circle and prepare members to deal effectively with what remains of unfinished business.

TRIBUTE TO FAMILY CAREGIVERS

Primary caregivers are those responsible for bathing, grooming, controlling medications, supervising diet, helping elderly people exercise and/or dealing with problems of incontinence. Sometimes primary caregivers are professionals — sometimes they are spouses, adult children, other family members or friends. These "nonprofessionals" often become practical nurses without a license — or pay. Yet they earn the respect of professionals. These individuals deserve all possible recognition, and belong to the "Caregivers Hall of Fame."

Many untrained family caregivers start out heavy on CARE and light on TECHNIQUE. Some learn nursing skills and emergency first-aid by attending classes; others learn by following suggestions made by doctors and other professionals; and still others learn from experience. Most turn out to be highly competent.

It is not the purpose of this book to present nursing techniques involved in primary caregiving. A publication that does an excellent job of this is CAREGIVING: HELPING AN AGING LOVED ONE. This is an AARP book published by Scott-Foresman and Co., 1865 Miner Street, Des Plaines, IL 60016.

SUMMARY

1. The foundation for success in helping aging parents often lies in building and maintaining as many healthy relationships as possible within the family circle over a period of years.

2. A family that communicates openly is often a family that will do well when dealing with unfinished business.

3. Family leadership is a challenge among siblings that requires special skills.

FAMILY STUDY #3

Communication Opportunities for Gary

Gary and his wife Hilda received some unnerving news late last night. Gary's older sister called to say their father had been hospitalized with what appeared to be a stroke. She added that their mother was doing well under the circumstances. Gary thanked his sister, knowing the leadership role she had so frequently played, and told her that he would call her back the following day.

Gary spent a sleepless night trying to figure out what action to take. As a child, he was taught to subdue his emotions because "men are supposed to be strong." Gary is considered a poor communicator by his co-workers and his family. Although he loves both his father and mother deeply, he has never been able to express his feelings.

Gary admits (to himself) that he has "the guilts" because, although he lives only an hour away from his parents (about the same as his older sister), he has communicated infrequently and permitted his sister to carry the big load.

PART I

Listed below are some options Gary is considering. Knowing his communication problem, which options is he likely to take?

1. Visit his father in the hospital immediately. Tell him that he is a great father.

2. Take his mother and older sister out to lunch and talk openly about how much the family means to him.

3. Provide leadership for a family meeting to discuss family support for the future.

4. Apologize to his older sister for not playing a stronger role in the past and promising to do better in the future.

5. Talk to Hilda as well as a professional counselor about his inability to communicate openly.

PART II

Suppose Gary does not follow through on any of the above, what additional options would you recommend?

_____

_____

_____

_____

_____

_____

_____

_____

_____

Compare your views by turning to pages 200–201.

FAMILY STUDY #4   **Which Letter Should Mrs. Snow Send?**

Mrs. Snow, a widow of five years, lives near her mother in the West and has always enjoyed their relationship. She is becoming concerned, however, about how much longer her mother will be able to live alone in the old family home. Recent signals that cause this concern are (1) not eating properly, (2) confusion over taking prescribed pills, and (3) unsteadiness on her feet. Last week Mrs. Snow arranged for her mother to wear a "beeper" in case she needed to summon immediate help.

So far, Mrs. Snow has handled all the little things (like arranging for repairs around the house and paying bills) by herself. She is worried, however, about future problems of a more serious nature and does not want to take the full responsibility herself.

There are three other siblings, all younger than Mrs. Snow. James is an insurance agent in New York, Jerry is a lawyer in Florida, and Jeff is a professor in Tennessee. All have families living at home. Her brothers have offered very little assistance (including money), and communication has been sporadic. What bothers Mrs. Snow is that they all seem to take her for granted. Without discussing the matter, they seem to assume she will remain close by, not remarry, and accept responsibility for all forms of care for their mother. Mrs. Snow admits to herself that she might be receptive to having her mother live with her, but she feels her brothers need to accept more leadership. She is tired of giving them a free ride and being taken for granted.

In a bold effort to correct the situation, Mrs. Snow has composed two letters to send to her brothers. The first takes a soft approach (her normal style) and discusses the signals she is receiving and the impending need for a major decision about increased care options. In this letter she expresses her fears. The second letter takes a more assertive posture and outlines a plan for a family meeting where all members can discuss the issues face to face. Uncharacteristically, she sets a deadline of 90 days for such a meeting to take place in their mother's home.

Which letter would you suggest Mrs. Snow send and why? Write your answer, and then match it with the interpretation on page 201.

_____

_____

_____

_____

_____

_____

_____

_____

_____

3

Do It For Love But Know What You Are Doing

"Death is not the greatest loss in life. The greatest loss is what dies inside us while we live."
Norman Cousins

Regardless of how successful you may be in converting the care of an elderly parent into a family affair, it is the one-on-one relationship you create and maintain between yourself and the loved one that counts most. The more wholesome the relationship, the less stress and guilt there will be from either end. The more enjoyable the relationship, the more each individual will benefit. Love is the secret ingredient but there are many other rewards.

It must be recognized, of course, not all key relationships are between aging individuals and their adult children. Many seniors have loving and significant relationships with spouses, brothers and sisters, grandchildren, friends,

29

neighbors, and even professional caretakers. Sometimes non-family relationships are the most important of all.

Mrs. Gray, age 83, has a loving and devoted family, but her most important relationship is with her boyfriend, Alvin.

Mr. Star, a widower now age 75, has no complaints about the way he is treated by family members, but the relationship he treasures most is with his neighbor and golfing buddy, Rex.

Mrs. Jarvis is not unhappy about the attention she receives from her three children, but it is her neighbor, Sally, that she would miss most.

It is also true that not all parents have the ability or desire to create and maintain meaningful non-family relationships. Because of this, some parents fall back on their children before they need to do so. It is unfortunate when this happens, especially when there is little love involved. Yet, even without love, it is possible for adult children to give extensive care to their parents. They may offer care out of guilt, filial devotion, or lack of information about options.

When hateful parents need care, an adult child can provide it through community support systems, or give it themselves, and still feel no love. In the vast majority of cases, however, care is freely given on the basis of love. During this period of unfinished business, relationships become stronger and more enjoyable. Most guilt feelings are left behind and lives are enriched. The challenge to both adult children and aging parents is to make this happen.

PARENT-CHILD RELATIONSHIPS ARE COMPLEX   Although child-parent relationships are often treasured beyond words, they are frequently emotionally charged and highly sensitive. Each relationship is unique. Even families with warm, loving and healthy feelings, do not have them all the time. At one extreme a domineering parent my intimate, manipulate, and/or use an adult child. The result is a tug of war that often damages the relationship beyond repair. At the other extreme, a child may ignore, manipulate, and mistreat a parent. The result is that both the adult child and the parent suffer a great loss. Most relationships fall somewhere between these two extremes.

RELATIONSHIP STRAINS   Once an adult child and aging parent enter the "unfinished business phase", pressures on both parties can increase. The push and pull on relationships can accelerate. It is all part of the process to clear up the unfinished business that accumulates as the senior family member grows older. The aging process increases parental needs, thus placing additional pressure on adult children. Aging itself puts new pressures on the parent, and it is important for adult children to acknowledge and accept this.

> When Marsha's mother broke her hip, additional strains were placed on her and she was resentful. Marsha had just gotten her children through college and on their own and now this. For the first few months Marsha felt that life was unfair. Then, thanks to a friend, she joined a community support group of adult children faced with similar problems. It didn't take long for Marsha to learn that her situation was not uncommon.

Even in the best of adult child-aging parent relationships, stress will exist. Some of the stress factors are listed below. How to deal with them will come later.

MONEY STRESS If you or other family members are providing financial assistance to an aging parent, there can be a strain on your budget which will be reflected in your attitude. At the same time the parent may feel strained because of the increased dependency. In contrast, if the aging parent is well off financially, the adult children may have ideas about how that money should be spent, or have plans for it themselves. The presence of wealth can, itself, be stress-producing.

It is important to acknowledge that money and/or possessions do affect relationships. As an antidote to the pressures that can develop, open communication is essential. In the short term, aging parents need to consider their own needs in order to take care of as much unfinished business as possible while they are still competent. In the long term, it is natural for them to be involved in the distribution of any estate that may exist. Wills, trusts, powers of attorney, and Letter's of Instruction are all part of this and will be dealt with later in this book. The important thing is to understand that pushing financial matters into the background will not only increase the stress on both sides, but also postpone critical parts of unfinished business.

STRESS CAUSED BY SELF-ISOLATION In addition to normal misunderstandings that occur when there is not enough open communication, some aging parents may isolate themselves at the very time they need most to communicate with their family (or friends). For example, if a family fails to discuss ahead of time the problems connected with unfinished business, an aging parent may attempt to shoulder their burdens alone. If stress is to be held to a minimum, it is important to share any concerns *before* a crisis occurs. Some adult children refrain from discussing aging issues with their parents for a variety of reasons. Some fear they may infringe upon their parents sense of independence. This can introduce additional stress into a relationship. It is far better to write, call, and visit regularly so that aging and future concerns can be introduced informally over a period of time.

DECISION-MAKING STRESS   The decision-making process almost always has a "pressure quotient" for both those who make the decision and those affected by it. Aging parents may find the process quite difficult as decisions often affect their health, home, income, and/or future independence. Most adult children can sense this stress and want to help their parents reach satisfactory and comfortable decisions. This can be difficult because the problem of motivating aging parents to make decisions is a role often alien to adult children.

HEALTH STRESS   Deteriorating health creates stress (pain) for both the ailing individuals and those who must observe the process. Fear of the future adds fuel to the fire. Will there be increasingly serious health problems? Will adequate medical help be available? Will it be costly? Will it change lives drastically? Who will be the final caretaker? Will all members of the family provide support? The questions outnumber the answers — and stress often accelerates as the end of unfinished business comes into view.

REDUCING STRESS   There are three ways to face the stress that unfinished business creates. The first is to ignore the problem and suffer some form of guilt the rest of your life; a second is to give in to the stress. By far the best is to accept the challenge brought on by unfinished business, and work to reduce stress to a minimum. The temptation to ignore the aging in someone you love is natural, but with planning, utilization of community support groups, and regular communication, assisting an aging parent can be comforting and enriching. A first step may be to learn how to release some stress (even though you cannot fully eliminate all of it).

HANDS-ON CARE vs. OTHER FORMS OF SUPPORT

Some adult children, mostly women, find they have the skills, and it is within their comfort zones to provide their parents with personal care such as help in bathing, dressing, food preparation, etc. Factors involved in making a decision to provide "hands-on" care include time available, health, career commitments, and other responsibilities. Those unable to provide "hands-on" care can and should find other forms of support to make their contribution. Other support can be recalled from the word SAFE.

Substitutes: Other people, (family members, neighbors, friends, and/or professionals) can be found to provide personal care. A few may perform services on a volunteer basis; others will require compensation.

Arranging community support: Adult children should investigate the various forms of support available within the community. Some services are free. Others are not.

Financial: Many adult children, especially those who live far away are in a position to provide financial support and do so willingly as part of their contribution.

Emotional: Some children who are unable to provide other forms of support make their contributions through visitations, telephone calls, and written communciations.

There is always a contribution that an adult child, close friend, or other family member can make. Whatever it may turn out to be, the individual should not feel "the guilts" because another may appear to be contributing more.

PROTECTING YOURSELF WHEN THINGS GET TOUGH It is seldom easy to maintain a "normal" relationship with an elderly parent or friend who is slipping physically or mentally. This is especially true when there is only one child involved and the relationship dependency is high. Still, the primary goal should be to protect your own physical and mental health as much as possible, because your strength will be needed more as you complete the unfinished business that lies ahead. To help protect yourself during this period (which may last for years) the following check list may serve as a guide.

PROTECTING YOURSELF AGAINST STRESS

When providing support for an elderly person (it may or may not include personal care) starts to get you down, there are many steps you can take to protect yourself. Check those that fall into your comfort zone. As you do this, keep in mind that there are community support groups you could join and if necessary, professional help. You are never totally alone.

☐ Use the "flipside technique," that is, turn the problem you are having with an aging individual over and try to see the humor in it. If you can find just a little humor in the situation, it will help you survive.

☐ Count your blessings. Back away from the intensity of the problem and look at the more positive things you have going for you. Count your winners as well as your losers.

☐ Rely on the "one day at a time" technique.

☐ Talk the problem out with a friend and later do something nice for that friend to repay him or her for being such a good listener.

☐ See your minister, priest, or rabbi for spiritual guidance.

☐ View yourself as an assistant to the elderly individual; this may help you remember that the more you help them help themselves, the better it will be for them and the less pressure on you.

PROTECTING YOURSELF AGAINST STRESS (cont.)

☐ Complete reading this book and use it as a guide for future support and ideas.

☐ Take a mini-vacation. It frequently can give you a better perspective.

☐ Discuss the strain you are feeling with the elderly person and ask for suggestions on how to reduce it.

☐ Start seeing your aging parent or friend less but stay longer; or shorten your visits. Sometimes a variation on visits is helpful.

☐ Ask another family member or community resource to assume more of the responsibility.

☐ Start exercising daily.

☐ Become involved in a special leisure activity.

☐ Search for ways to stop worrying about problems beyond your control.

☐ Develop a new non-family relationship or enhance an old one, so there is a better balance between your family and non-family relationships.

☐ Seek counseling if you feel the need.

☐ Others:

_____

_____

You may know about a situation where one spouse (healthy at the beginning) devoted so much time and energy to the care of the other spouse that she or he also became ill and neither had the other to lean on. This is why your own physical and mental health should receive top priority. The above ideas are only suggestions. You may find other steps to take, but whatever is required, do it. You are more important than you may realize!

DEALING WITH HIGHLY DEMANDING PARENTS

"Mellow" means to become more understanding and sympathetic. Some aging parents mellow. Others do not. Adult children of demanding parents need to find ways to deal with their special problem and work toward completing unfinished business under these more difficult conditions. Here are some suggestions that may help:

Immunize your emotions. Some domineering and highly critical parents are more demanding with their words than their hearts. Most do not expect things to change in their favor — they just need to complain because the world did not live up to their expectations. Seek the underlying message and let unfounded complaints roll off your shoulder.

Embrace the tough love approach. "Tough love" is a genuine form of love. It means you can get tough (stand up for yourself) yet continue to love the other party as before. For example, if an over-demanding parent starts to be unreasonable, you might say, "I am unwilling to stay with you when you are like this." *Then leave.*

Your words and action may communicate to the parent that she or he will lose your "ear" if improvements are not made. "Tough love" may be necessary if you are to accomplish tasks for the benefit of your parent and still maintain your own mental health.

Protect your other relationships. Sometimes an adult child will become so intimidated and engrossed in a parent relationship that he or she will make the mistake of ignoring other relationships. A demanding parent makes your other relationships more important, not less. There is another danger. Although you need the "ear" that a spouse or close friend can provide, that person should not be bombarded with your aging parent problem.

ATTITUDE CAN MAKE THE DIFFERENCE

As you make your contribution to the lives of your aging parents, the following tips may help you to remain positive.

Tip #1: *Remember that with the right attitude everthing you learn about helping an older person can contribute to your ability to age well.* It is difficult to learn about aging from a distance. Close encounters may be difficult at times, but they can contribute to your personal growth. You may learn a new meaning to life. You may learn how to overcome other problems you face.

Tip #2: *Do what you do because you want to and not because it has been forced upon you.* This attitude may not be easy to assume, but it can cause you to benefit in other ways. For example, doing what you do because you want to makes your gift more valuable. It has a way of uplifting those on the receiving end. This, in turn, can make you feel better about yourself.

Tip #3: *Give other family members the space they need to create beautiful relationships on their own.* Jealousies may creep into relationships. For example, you may do more for a parent than your sister or brother, but one of them may appear to be favored by your parent. Do not let this damage your relationship. Jealousy may rear its ugly head but you do not have to give it status. The more love present within a family, the more everyone will benefit, especially the aging parent.

Tip #4: *Refuse to become involved in conflict situations where you have had no previous involvement.* Should a conflict develop between others in your family, remain outside it. Your primary concern is to keep a good relationship with your aging parent and the other family members. By taking sides you may diminish the future contributions you could make.

SUMMARY

1. Relationships between adult children and parents often become more stressful during the period of unfinished business.

2. Adult children need to protect themselves during these periods. There are many "safety valves" available.

3. Dealing with demanding parents presents a special challenge. Different techniques and approaches are needed to help an adult child cope with this situation.

HELPING A REMAINING SPOUSE

Many adult children receive a traumatic introduction to unfinished business when they unexpectedly lose one parent. It is a critical and sensitive "shock period" that often brings a family closer together. But not always.

Sometimes, due to a lack of planning and solid communications, points of alienation are exposed: (1) a family member who was not fully involved in the final service arrangements might be hurt; (2) intolerance for the way in which one family member expresses her or his grief might be upsetting to another; (3) the manner in which the remaining parent is advised can become a bone of contention. Rather than being a period of understanding, reconciliation, and love, family relationships can become strained during this period and the remaining spouse suffers.

The biggest mistake is to shower the remaining mother or father with too much attention, protection, and/or advice. What is needed at this critical juncture is the time to grieve, remember, assess, and adjust. To quickly raise an umbrella of protection is a great disservice. Concern and support are helpful — but not too much. Otherwise an over-protection pattern for the unfinished business of the remaining spouse can continue for years.

Generally speaking, a widow or widower needs at least six months to make a satisfactory adjustment. During this period, time is required to allow the survivor to talk at length about the lost partner and other concerns. Adult children should remember that (1) being available is more important than making premature decisions, and (2) any responsibility assumed should be done on a temporary basis and returned to the living parent as soon as possible.

There are a number of major decisions that should be withheld until after the adjustment period. Some include: (1) a quick change in the living environment; (2) important financial decisions; (3) conclusions on the ability of the remaining spouse to live alone.

Eventually, the unfinished business of the remaining spouse must be dealt with, but only after an unpressured adjustment period has concluded. Unless this is provided, the living mother or father may not make the quality decisions she or he should be making.

FAMILY STUDY #5   Reverse Abuse

Mrs. King has always dominated her daughter Maria. When Maria comes by for her daily visit, Mrs. King berates her for insignificant slights. Although Maria and her mother have never had a really good mother-daughter relationship, further deterioration is taking place.

Maria is distraught but seems unable to turn the tables. She feels that her mother's aging problems have made her mother more difficult. She wants her mother to recognize her devotion but she gets nothing but rebuffs in return. This is even more frustrating because her brother, who does nothing, is lauded by Mrs. King. Maria still wants to please her mother, but is increasingly depressed about their relationship.

Assume you are conducting a support group for adult children with difficult parents. What recommendations would you make to Maria? Write your comments below and then turn to page 201.

_____

_____

_____

_____

_____

_____

FAMILY STUDY #6   **John and Heidi**

Heidi was waiting when John returned from his Saturday game of golf. "Honey, we've got something serious to talk about. After your shower, I want you to give me thirty minutes of your time."

Heidi started things off reviewing how they were doing coping with the pressures both were under. With three children in college the financial pressure was something they had adjusted to rather well, since both were working. The constant stream of small problems from the children was not insurmountable either, but what was getting to both of them was the problem of dealing with John's aging mother and Heidi's aging mother and father.

Heidi said, "We are not the only ones under intense pressure from having children on one side and parents on the other. Some of my friends at work are in worse shape. The good news, however, is that we can do something about it. I discovered that starting next Tuesday night a support group at church is forming, composed entirely of adults who have aging parents. I want to attend. Will you go with me? There will be eight two-hour sessions, and the leader is experienced and has conducted successful groups in other churches."

"I don't know", replied John, "if you can convince me that it will actually relieve some of the pressure and help us do a better job with our parents, maybe, but I don't want to air our dirty linen in public. What we do with our aging parents is our business —what others do is theirs. I have this terrible feeling that the more we know about the problem the worse things will get. Sometimes it is better not to know what is ahead."

If you were Heidi, how might you convince John that attendance at such a support group would make the future easier and brighter and that children and aging parents would benefit? Write your answer and then make a comparison by turning to page 202.

4

Both Parent And Child Can Benefit

In maintaining good relationships with older people, nothing makes more sense than the Mutual Reward Theory. This simple idea gives unfinished business both meaning and promise.

The Mutual Reward Theory (MRT) states that all human relationships become stronger and last longer when there is a good and reasonable *exchange of rewards*. When two people of any age — family or non-family — have a frequent and enjoyable "reward exchange," the relationship itself becomes healthier and both parties benefit. It is a win/win situation!

It is a simple premise that is difficult to refute. If you visit an aging parent or friend in a nursing home, and because you are a good listener, the resident has an opportunity to

43

communicate joys, concerns, and complaints, then you are providing that person with a psychological *reward*. On the way out you may discover that you feel better yourself because you have satisfied your "giving nature" (perhaps even dissipated a little guilt); so you, too, have received a reward. Both you and the person you visited are winners! MRT is working!

MRT works in business, with your children, in other personal relationships, and within family circles. The ideal situation for the application of this theory, however, is between adult children and their aging parents. The timing and application may seem awkward, but the rewards to both parties can be greater.

THE ROLE REVERSAL MYTH

Some individuals adhere to the role reversal idea. This idea states that parents take care of their children when they are young, and the same children (when they become adults) will take care of their parents who, in a sense, *become children.*

This "role reversal" assumption should not be made for three good reasons: (1) it is unhealthy to think of parents as children (no matter how fragile they become), because it denies them the significant roles they have already played in life; (2) the assumption is demeaning and can cause excessive "do gooding" for an aging parent when empowerment is needed; (3) the role reversal idea gets in the way of MRT because treating a parent as a child prevents the parent from giving adult rewards they are still capable of giving.

THE INTER-GENERATIONAL PAY-BACK PHILOSOPHY

It is natural and encouraging to know that many children, after they become adults, feel obligated to pay their parents back for the many rewards they received while growing up. This is MRT working on a delayed basis. But, it is a serious mistake for adult children to think there are not some current rewards they can also receive and enjoy from their parents. Parents receive many rewards from their children (especially love) as they raise them; the same children can receive rewards by providing increased attention to their aging parents. This "pay-back" philosophy offers the promise of balancing out the giving over the life span of the aging parent.

GIVING IS ITS OWN REWARD

Many people have such a deep capacity for love that they can give and give with few expectations for themselves. Giving for these people is its own reward. It is a wonderful arrangement, but in most relationships the constant "giver" but non-receiver eventually feels (at one level or another) "put upon." When this happens, there is the danger that the relationship will deteriorate and the giving will be withdrawn, or the "giver" will say, "enough is enough." This situation can occur when an adult child is operating under the pay-back philosophy and is trying to balance out the many rewards received as a child.

Research indicates that some adult children operate on this theory because they feel they can never repay their parents adequately, no matter how hard they try. Sometimes, they over-give to the point they stifle parents, injure other relationships, and create resentment in themselves.

Even when immediate rewards seem to be unnecessary in a relationship, such rewards are nice to receive; they still contribute to a stronger, more enjoyable relationship. On the next page is a hypothetical *reward exchange matrix* that could exist between anyone and an aging person. The purpose of this matrix is to demonstrate that there are many rewards that can be given *from both sides of the relationship.*

MONEY AS A PART OF THE MUTUAL REWARD IDEA

If you see a bumper sticker on an expensive R.V. that reads *We are having fun spending our children's inheritance*, you can guess that the subject of money has received at least some consideration in the development of the relationships between the owners and their children. If you hear the phrase *How can I protect my inheritance without generating guilt feelings*, you can sense that money has been introduced as an issue between an adult child and his or her parents.

REWARD EXCHANGE MATRIX

Listed in the left column are some rewards adult children (and others) can provide to aging family members. In the right column are some of the rewards that senior members can provide to family members and their friends. THE MORE REWARDS EACH PARTY RECEIVED, THE HEALTHIER THE RELATIONSHIP WILL BE AND THE LONGER IT WILL LAST.

Adult Children/Others		Senior Family Members
The receiving and giving of love.	⟷	The receiving and giving of love.
Learning about family history and certain qualities they may have inherited.	⟷	Opportunity to reminisce and relive important aspects of their lives.
Absence of guilt — feeling like a "good child."	⟷	Receiving special care and attention.
Learning first hand about the aging process.	⟷	Taking pleasure in being a good senior role model.
Dispersing myths about aging.	⟷	Sensing (with pleasure) that children are maturing well.
Awareness of living a healthy lifestyle in preparation for a better retirement later.	⟷	Feeling good about adult children taking good care of themselves so they can take over family leadership.
Having "model of courage" to emulate.	⟷	Pride in being a "Master Senior" and good survivor.
Self-respect that comes from fulfilling a responsibility to parents.	⟷	Knowing family is grateful for your contributions.

REWARD EXCHANGE MATRIX (cont.)

Adult Children/Others		Senior Family Members
New awareness of the importance of family.	⟷	Knowing you are helping to pull family closer together.
Financial rewards — enjoying the fruits of parents' labor.	⟷	Enjoyment from realizing accumulated possessions are appreciated.
Having your children benefit from contact with grandparents.	⟷	Receiving the joy of a child's love.
The opportunity to "counsel" on important family matters.	⟷	The opportunity to discuss matters of deep concern.
Understanding the past.	⟷	Validation of values.
Knowing that unfinished business of being taken care of.	⟷	Knowing that unfinished business is being taken care of.

Other rewards:

_____

_____

_____

_____

Other rewards:

_____

_____

_____

_____

The possibilities of a good reward exchange between younger and senior family members offers great promise if understood and practiced. Although performing "care tasks" because of a sense of obligation from past rewards is to be admired, immediate rewards are still available and when enjoyed the relationship benefits. Both parties benefit now, no matter what has occurred in the past.

Because money is often a "touchy subject" in family circles, it would be tempting to leave the subject out of this book. This would, of course, be unrealistic since the passing of wealth and cherished belongings between generations is an important part of *unfinished business*.

AGING PARENTS' VIEW ON MONEY

One can overhear expressions similar to these among many senior family members:

> "I wish I had spent more money along the way because I have never seen a hearse with a luggage rack on top."
>
> "The thing that bothers me most about leaving money to my kids is that they have never learned the value of a dollar. I might as well blow it myself before it is too late."
>
> "I know I shouldn't say it, but I honestly get the feeling sometimes that our kids are waiting for us to die, so they can get their hands on our money."

Such expressions aside, most senior members who possess a degree of wealth know that their money gives them a sense of power and helps them maintain a degree of independence. Such wealth can help provide better care during later years. Most aging parents know, however, that money doesn't replace love. As a result, most wish to use their money wisely. They want it to take them through whatever lies ahead, and then, whatever may be left over needs to be distributed in a fair manner. This does not mean that many aging parents will never use money to secure attention, favors, and love while they are still around. Some will. And, it is not unusual for parents to distribute their wealth in proportion to the attention that they receive. The problem with this approach is that money may replace love, and relationships can become distorted.

It cannot be denied, however, that money, wealth and possessions can constitute a reward to adult children from aging parents, and if financial incentives motivate adult children to do more for their parents, it is not an unworthy emphasis.

ADULT CHILD'S VIEW ON MONEY

From the view of the adult child, money may play either a major or insignificant role. The presence of wealth, however, is a factor that can influence relationships, as the following comments indicate.

> "My folks are sitting on a batch of money, so I'm not going to do anything to hurt my chances of inheriting some of it."
>
> "I don't want my parents to go without anything they need and can enjoy, but I hope there is some left over for us kids."
>
> "It bothers me that I find myself doing things for my folks because of a possible inheritance; but, at least, I am honest about it."

Regardless of what one may hear, most adult children put love, care, and other emotional and psychological elements ahead of money. However, it may be best to openly accept the fact that wealth, through inheritance, is a legitimate reward for taking care of unfinished business. It is only hoped that the "money reward" is wrapped in integrity, concern, and love.

It is, of course, important to be aware of all possible rewards (including money) that are available for exchange between adult children and their parents. To have such rewards recognized and appreciated is another matter. Here are some tips for both adult children and seniors.

**MAKING
MRT WORK**

| Tips To Adult Children |

1. If any childhood misunderstandings remain between you and a parent, it is probably best to "forget them." This is not an appropriate time to dump old conflicts on an aging parent.

2. Learn to ignore negative comments such as "nobody loves me anymore," "getting older is not worth it," and "wait until you get to be my age." Switch quickly to more positive subjects.

3. Continue to develop as a person so you can meet your own needs as well as theirs.

4. If you decide to give up a few of your own freedoms to contribute to an aging parent, accept it gracefully and recognize that it can help.

5. Recognize that quality time with an aging parent is often better than long hours. Really be *present* when you are at his or her side.

6. Provide all the rewards you can; learn to value those you receive.

7. Learn to be lovingly firm.

8. If possible, plan a vacation or special outing where you can take your aging parent with you.

9. Keep in mind that a rested, positive adult child has more to give.

10. Anything you can do to keep an aging parent from feeling she or he has been "put on the shelf" will enhance communication and give her or him courage to do more for themselves.

11. Try to remember that the more rewards you give and receive from your special relationship with a parent, the more positive you will be with other people in your life.

12. Confide in your parents and seek their advice. Don't worry about causing them concern. They would rather be informed and involved than be left to guess.

13. Show your love.

Tips For Mature Parents

1. Keep in mind that younger people live their lives in a world different from the one you knew at their age.

2. Give them all the space possible and try not to impose your values upon them.

3. Keep communication lines open.

4. The more you show your appreciation to adult children for the rewards they provide, the more positive they will be about dealing with unfinished business. Showing appreciation is a reward.

5. Stay involved in the decision-making process concerning your life; but if an adult child contributes, give him or her the reward of a sincere compliment.

6. Try not to overdo it, but be comfortable sharing your aging experiences and needs, so that adult children can better "understand."

7. Maintain a sense of humor so you will be an enjoyable person to be around.

8. Develop and maintain a network of friends so you will not become overly dependent on your adult children.

9. Stay as independent as possible, but learn how to accept help (rewards) and be grateful for it.

10 Mend fences quickly when necessary (there is nothing wrong with an aging parent apologizing to an adult child).

11. As far as possible, keep in touch with the real world. Let others know so they can "read" your current capabilities correctly.

12. Enlighten your adult children about your financial status and your wishes for your aging years. It is difficult for adult children to provide the "right" rewards unless they know what you really want.

13. Show your love.

As one incorporates MRT into his or her behavioral patterns it is good to keep in mind that the win/win philosophy is not an automatic even-exchange arrangement. MRT is more like a checking account where you make deposits and withdrawals (both rewards) and the interest that accumulates makes both parties even bigger winners. Sometimes, of course, one person will make a big deposit while the other makes a small one. Best of all, there is no time framework — you may accept a reward now and not return it until a later date. Of course, providing rewards to aging individuals always holds the danger of waiting too long and the person is not around to receive the reward you could have provided much sooner...and really wanted to!

SUMMARY

1. Although MRT can work in all relationships, it can be especially helpful between an adult child and aging parent.

2. The key to making MRT successful is the balance of the reward exchange between both parties.

3. Love is the most precious of all rewards that can be given or received. Money is also a reward and should be dealt with openly.

THE CATALYTIC ROLE OF GRANDCHILDREN

Grandchildren can contribute greatly to family unity. Indeed, a grandchild is sometimes the only individual that can establish and maintain a healthy relationship between adult children and their aging parents. Still, even under excellent circumstances, things do not always go well. To enhance the significant role grandchildren can play, the following suggestions are made to both adult children (parents) and grandparents.

Suggestions for Parents	Suggestions for Grandparents
Set easy-to-understand rules when children are to be alone with grandparents.	Accept and respect the rules that are set down by parents.
Do not begrudge a beautiful child-grandparent relationship.	Always support the values and teachings of your adult children.
Do not discuss shortcomings of grandparents in front of a grandchild.	Do not discuss any family matter that a grandchild might misinterpret.
If grandparents see a grandchild infrequently, encourage the child to write letters, send drawings, etc. Also, include them in telephone conversations.	If separated from a grandchild, use the mails and telephone to keep in touch. Send frequent surprises.
When you permit a child to visit a grandparent alone, view it as a growth period for the child, but set visitation rules ahead of time.	Always get parent approval for special gifts (including money). Be a cautious guardian even if the grandchild pressures you to be otherwise.
Do not hesitate to discuss the child-grandparent relationship openly.	Try not to overdo with presents or treats.

FAMILY STUDY #7   Warren's Disturbing Condition

In a way, it is all understandable. Warren, at age 75, lost
two wives he dearly loved to the same illness, and was
forced into retirement before he was ready. Now he realizes
that he has failed to build good relationships with his two
children, Warren Jr. and Sandy. As a result, he broods over
the past and drinks heavily to forget it.

Last week, his son, suspecting that his father might be an
alcoholic, drove across town to pay him a surprise visit.
Warren, Jr. found the small apartment was a mess, his
father was filthy, and drunk to the point he was unable to
communicate logically.

After cleaning his father up and putting him to bed,
Warren Jr. decided he needed to talk to his sister about
the problem. This resulted in a family meeting (spouses
included) where the situation was discussed. They discussed
in detail the responsibilities they had. They decided if they
took no action immediately, the situation would get even
worse, and they would add to their guilt feelings.

If you were Warren Jr. or Sandy, what action, if any, would
you take? What would you hope to achieve? Is it too late for
an MRT relationship? Write your answers in the spaces
below and compare with suggestions on page 203.

_____

_____

_____

_____

_____

_____

_____

FAMILY STUDY #8 **Communication Compatibility**

Mrs. Askew lost her husband to cancer last year. She had
stopped working in order to care for him. The several
months following his death were a tough period for her.
When things settled down a little, Mrs. Askew started
spending time with her mother who was a resident in a
local nursing home on 24 hour care.

Mrs. Askew soon discovered that her visits were
therapeutic for both she and her mother. Somehow, they
were communicating on a new level. For the first time in
years they were enjoying each other. Mrs. Askew provided
her mother with some laughs; but more importantly, shared
an opportunity to discuss problems and fears. In return,
Mrs. Askew enjoyed learning some intriguing family history,
especially about her own youth. Also, she learned more
about her mother's deep and beautiful spirituality. In
discussing her new relationship with her mother to a friend,
she commented: "It is really amazing how one who is so
physically frail can provide such high quality communication. It was very difficult to lose my husband and stop working. Whatever help I have been to my mother, she has been
more help to me. After all these years, our relationship is
mutually rewarding."

During some of their lighter periods of conversation, her
mother's roommate would participate. A charming lady, she
often talked about her son Jerry. Then one day Mrs. Askew
met Jerry. They hit it off immediately. A few weeks later
when they were visiting their mothers, Jerry invited
Mrs. Askew to have dinner. They discovered they had much
in common. Jerry had recently lost his wife of many years,
and honestly enjoyed the rewards of communication with his
mother. Three months following their first meeting, Jerry
asked Mrs. Askew to marry him.

Please respond to the following questions.

1. Why do you feel it took so long for Mrs. Askew to enjoy and benefit from communicating with her mother?

_____

_____

_____

_____

_____

2. Because both Mrs. Askew and Jerry discovered a mutually rewarding relationship through frequent communication with elderly mothers, is this an indication they could build a mutually rewarding relationship in their own marriage?

_____

_____

_____

_____

_____

Compare your suggestions with those of the author on page 203.

5

The Process Of Turning Things Over

"The more complete one's life is, the more...one's creative capacities are fulfilled, the less one fears death...People are not afraid of death per se, but the incompleteness of their lives."
Lisl Marburg Goodman

A transfer of power or authority takes place in a business when the president retires or resigns. It happens in politics when a new candidate wins an election, and it also occurs within family circles. As one generation puts the final touches on unfinished business, a new generation is usually waiting to assume family responsibilities. One way or another, most families perpetuate themselves.

In some cases, however, there is a "wrenching away of authority" by members of the younger generation before senior members are ready to relinquish it. This often happens when aging parents are too reluctant or too stubborn about "turning things over," or perhaps there is

57

too little communication taking place. At the other extreme, aging parents can be anxious and willing to wind up the process of unfinished business, but nobody is willing to "take over the reins."

Each family must handle the transfer in their own way. Each transition is based upon such factors as number of children, the size of the estate (if any), family cohesiveness, and the style of aging parents. This Chapter is designed to act as a guide to facilitate the transition.

SLOW EDUCATION AND PREPARATION OR A LAST MINUTE TURNOVER?

There are basically two ways to complete a transfer of power: (1) via the slow, orderly process of communication, and (2) the delayed approach, where aging parents prepare everything on paper (wills, trusts, etc.) and turn things over at the last minute or after they have gone. We will call these two strategies PLAN A and PLAN B.

Example of Plan A:

Mr. and Mrs. Spencer, after gaining approval from their two children who were less interested, started educating their daughter, Noreen, to "take over." They started soon after celebrating their 50th wedding anniversary. Mr. Spencer devoted hours helping Noreen understand their modest investment portfolio and other financial matters. Mrs. Spencer worked with Noreen on the distribution of family possessions and other final details such as a Letter of Instruction (see page 176). A Will and Trust had been completed previously with the help of a lawyer. Noreen would be the executrix and trustee. Mr. and Mrs. Spencer had the following goals in mind: (1) free themselves of financial and other responsibilities ahead of time so they could enjoy their last years with greater freedom and peace of mind; (2) to give Noreen a chance to assume power while they were still around to provide guidance; (3) to bring the family closer together by communicating to all openly in advance.

FAMILY POWER

Families — weak or strong — derive power from three primary sources. First is the way in which the family tradition is preserved. Some families have a strong desire to preserve what has been handed down to them and pass it along to the next generation. These family members are often willing to wrap their love in traditional time-consuming activities (such as holiday rituals), to keep family ties strong.

Second is the personality power of the family leaders. Often those with a desire to maintain family traditions are the strongest leaders. Some families enjoy great family leaders for two or three generations and then, failing a strong personality to carry the torch, grow weak.

A third source of power is wealth. The intergenerational transfer of power is frequently wrapped around the wealth of a previous generation. Such wealth can take many forms: security or investment portfolios, a family business, property, valuable heirlooms, collectables, vacation homes, etc. Obviously, the more wealth one generation has, the more complex it is to transfer it. Thus, in many families, the transfer of wealth becomes a significant part of unfinished business.

Example of Plan B:

Mr. and Mrs. Slade have a modest estate similar to that of the Spencers, but they have decided to take care of the transfer of power in writing rather than open communication. Through their lawyer (who will be both executor and trustee), they have not only completed a Will and Trust, but also a Letter of Instruction covering other final details. Rather than deal directly with their children, Mr. and Mrs. Slade feel a "quick paper turnover" at the end will be more beneficial to all. This does not mean less communication on other matters. It simply means that the "good times" need not be interrupted with financial and other problems. Mr. and Mrs. Slade, as do the Spencers, work as a team so that when one goes first the other will be in "full power." Mr. and Mrs. Slade have adopted their strategy to reach the following goals: (1) gain more attention and respect from their children and grandchildren by avoiding serious matters and concentrating on "good times;" (2) avoid possible family conflicts by refusing to delegate powers to one child and not to others; (3) save themselves the time connected with any "turnover" process, plus the disappointment that might occur should the child not follow through as hoped.

Please keep Plan A (Spencers) and Plan B (Slades) in mind as you evaluate the concepts of this chapter. You will be invited (as an adult child or aging parent) to select a plan of your own at the end of this section. In preparation, if one of the following ideas appeals to you, place a check in the appropriate square.

☐ **Temporary Transfers of Power Constitute Good Preparation.** Thus far, we have looked at the "power transfer process" through prior planning, (i.e. accomplished slowly ahead of time with open communication, or done by advanced "paper planning" for turnover when the time is right).

Temporary transfers may become necessary at any time regardless of the best laid plans. For example, if Mrs. Slade were widowed and found it necessary to have surgery, one of her three children might find it necessary to "take over" until she was back on her feet. Once recovered, Mrs. Slade could take back the powers she temporarily relinquished. If this happened, and Mrs. Slade was able to resume control, at least one child would be better prepared for the future. A temporary power transfer would fit better into Plan A than Plan B, because Plan A calls for a gradual transfer of power.

☐ **The Number One Son Tradition.** In Japan (and to a lesser extent in England), transferring power is made easy, because it is anticipated the oldest son will take over at the helm and continue to honor tradition. Often the oldest son is given additional education to help prepare him for his responsibilities. Other siblings are raised understanding what is to happen so parents with more than one child are not faced with a difficult decision.

The number one son tradition is not the case in most American families. It may be the major reason why Mr. and Mrs. Slade have decided not to turn things over in a gradual orderly manner. When two or more children are available, on what basis should they decide? Who is the best prepared? Most willing? Lives closest? Most trust-worthy? Should the decision be by consensus? Should a family meeting be held in an attempt to gain approval?

When the Spencer's selected Noreen as the number one daughter, did they alienate the other children? Did this, despite open communications, place Noreen in a difficult situation?

☐ **The Wrongful Assumption of Power.** A few adult children wrongfully assume power and "take over" when there is no verified medical need to do so, and power has not been freely given. This deprives their parents of freedom. This is most apt to occur after the loss of one spouse and before the remaining spouse has had a chance to recover. Sometimes "taking over" is encouraged by the remaining spouse because she or he is highly vulnerable to suggestions during this adjustment period.

Because both the Spencers and the Slades have a modest estate, it is possible (but unlikely) that one of their children could try to assume power to gain control over the distribution of the estate.

☐ **The Partnership Concept.** As you compare Plan A and Plan B, it is obvious that the Spencers took Noreen (and to a more limited extent their other children) into their confidence. As a partner, Noreen slowly became involved in decisions; and as she assumed more respon-sibility, the Spencers were more free to enjoy their last years together. Although the case does not specify, it is possible that Noreen received compensation for her "partnership" role. If so, this would be a reward that should be openly discussed with the other children to prevent jealousies. Do family partnerships work? Were the Slades smart not to select one child over others? Every family situation is different.

☐ **The Team Approach.** Although the risks are many, it is possible for aging parents to relinquish power to their children as a team. The biggest handicaps to this approach are proximity and communication. If the entire family lives in a small town, the possibility of success increases. If the family is scattered, the possibility of success decreases. Even under ideal circumstances, the risks are many, especially when a sizable estate is involved.

Should the Spencers have considered the team approach so that all three children would be equal partners to the transfer of power process? Despite possible geographical separations, could they have functioned as a "team"?

☐ **The Loss of Identity Consideration.** It is generally agreed among experts on aging that older people should try to keep a strong identity as long as possible. They should remain involved in family and community matters. To some, turning over family power signals their last role; to others, like the Spencers, it can mean release from responsibilities. The Spencers may feel that they can maintain their power roles even though all financial and others matters have been settled. But, are the Slades right? Is it really best for them to stay involved and in charge?

☐ **Power as a Burden That Damages Relationships.** We, of course, have no way of knowing how Noreen will react to becoming a "partner." Will she accept her new power as an opportunity and show new personal growth? Or might she see her responsibilities as a burden and think less of her parents? Might the Slades be right in thinking that their children might prefer a paper transfer without any extra responsibility now?

Perhaps the Slade children will eventually respect their parents more for giving them "extra years of freedom"?

☐ **The Communication Problem.** It is obvious that the Spencers also assume a responsibility when they started educating Noreen to "take over." Many communication sessions would be necessary — many questions would need to be answered. Apparently, the Spencers decided that the involvement would be good for many reasons. They may have felt it would build better relationships and increase the number of family gatherings. The rewards would far outweigh the time devoted. On the other hand, the Slades may have felt it would not be worth the communication efforts and the risk that misunderstandings might develop.

It would appear that the success of Plan A may depend upon the ability of the Spencers to communicate with Noreen and their other two children. If the relationship lines are open and frequent communication is enjoyed, it could be the superior plan. However, if all communication centered around financial matters and little time was devoted to "good times," the plan could fail. Communication could be the key. If the Spencers can use communication on financial matters to increase communication in other areas, then their goal of bringing the family closer together could work. The Slades apparently feel the risk of trying to accomplish this is too great, or else they do not want the extra involvement themselves.

☐ **The Possibility of Regrets and Remorse.** Many a father has turned over a business to a son or daughter only to regret it later because the adult child had a different "management" style. Turning over family power is also a risk that should be fully understood ahead of time. When aging parents are highly successful and skillful at managing financial (and other family) affairs, they may not be able to accept different performance levels by their offspring. In making such a transfer, they need to prepare themselves to be understanding and flexible, and have reasonable expectations.

In this respect, the Spencers have confidence in themselves. The Slades do not wish to take the risk.

☐ **Transfer of Power and the Mutual Reward Theory.** Adult children need to be prepared to accept power when received and ready to return power when it is best to do so. Aging parents, on the other hand, need to eventually transfer power to lessen their own responsibility and contribute to the future of the family. If done gracefully so that relationships remain loving and respectful, MRT is applicable.

Aging parents can receive many rewards: (1) achieve peace of mind by knowing that the family is in good hands; (2) relax knowing that their estate (if any) will be perpetuated; (3) enjoy the "turnover" process itself.

Adult children can also receive rewards: (1) they can benefit educationally from the "turnover" process; (2) they can get to know their parents better, and hopefully, respect them more; (3) whatever possessions might be involved can constitute tangible rewards.

Although it might appear that the application of MRT gives the advantage to Plan A (communications on financial matters and early "turnover" possibilities can be seen as rewards), this does not mean that the Slades cannot use the theory. In fact, by holding back on open discussions and other financial "turnovers" they might be able to make MRT work even better in other areas. For example, they can give more "fun" rewards because time is not being devoted to more serious unfinished business.

TAKEOVER EXERCISE*

Based on your analysis of Plan A and Plan B state your preference as an adult child.

I prefer Plan A for the following reasons:

_____

_____

I prefer Plan B for the following reasons:

_____

_____

Based upon your analysis, state your preference as a *senior family member.*

I prefer Plan A for the following reasons.

_____

_____

I prefer Plan B for the following reasons:

_____

_____

* As you complete this exercise, take into consideration all of the circumstances of your own family situation.

SUMMARY

1. The transfer of power between aging parents and their adult children (or other family circle members) is an important part of unfinished business. Sometimes the power transferred is symbolic and sometimes it can be a sizable estate.

2. The timing and manner of transfer is up to the aging parents. To gain freedom from responsibility, some start the "turnover" process early; others, to maintain a stronger identity, wait as long as possible. Either way, there are advantages and disadvantages.

3. When a transfer of power is handled gracefully, the mutual reward theory can come into play.

FAMILY STUDY #9 Turnover

It has been less than three months since John's father died unexpectedly from a heart problem. John is amazed at the strength his mother has shown in making adjustments. But yesterday was something else!

After John and his wife, Sally, had taken his mother out to dinner, she asked them to stay for a few minutes to discuss an important matter. She started the conversation by saying, "John, I devoted my life to your father and our family. Now it is time to be free and do what I want to do. I want to sell this home and move into a less-demanding condominium. I also want to turn all business matters over to someone I can trust. This will give me the freedom to travel, make new friends, and do the creative things that I always pushed into the background. Please call a family meeting to decide how I can best do this. If none of you kids want to take over, then let's designate an individual we all trust."

John feels like he is between a rock and a hard place. On one hand, he would like to assume the responsibility, but the demands on his time are too great. On the other hand, he doubts that he and his two sisters can agree on an outside individual to administer the sizable family estate. Getting everyone together to make a decision would be almost as difficult as gaining their approval and doing it himself.

List in the spaces below the steps you would recommend John take and then compare them to those listed on page 204.

_____

_____

_____

_____

_____

_____

_____

FAMILY STUDY #10   **Can of Worms**

Through hard work, good judgment, and luck, Mr. and Mrs. Evers, both in their seventies, have built a sizable estate. Most of the estate is tied up in a successful small business which they operated as partners until they retired last year.

Up to this point, their retirement has been less than successful because of their five children! Only one married daughter (with two children) who lives in the same community, has not given Mr. and Mrs. Evers problems. The remaining four have kept things unhappy. One son lives in another state and refuses to communicate. Two other sons divorced their home-town wives (whom Mr. and Mrs. Evers adored) and remarried divorced women with children who have made no effort to be a part of the family. Sally, the youngest, keeps coming home for "bail out" purposes.

Mrs. Evers is more compassionate and forgiving than her husband. She wants to divide their estate equally among the five children, and begin giving it annually to avoid heavy estate taxes. Her attitude is reflected in these comments: "My primary goal is to pull our family together, and I think one way to do this is to share our estate ahead of time. Sure, our kids haven't been perfect, but they are older now. If we share our estate, bit by bit, ahead of time, it could create a more harmonious atmosphere. We can do this and still have all the money we need to enhance our retirement years."

Mr. Evers had a different view. A believer in the Mutual Reward Theory, he feels the five children should share in the estate based on the rewards they have provided to his wife and himself in recent years. For example, Alice (the daughter who has stayed near them and contributed greatly) should receive the most. The others, especially Sally, should receive much less. On top of this, Mr. Evers is adamant that the distribution of their estate should occur through a will and/or trust *after* they have departed. This is his attitude: "If we start distributing our estate ahead of time based on the way we have been treated in recent years, we will open up a can of worms. Things will be worse than they are already. However, if it all happens after we are gone, each child will receive what he or she deserves, and we won't be around to hear the cries of dismay. Besides, we need to give them more time to decide just how important we are in the family structure. My idea is to keep them guessing about a possible inheritance until we know how much support and love they are willing to provide as we grow older."

Do you agree with Mrs. Evers or Mr. Evers? State your feelings below and then outline a compromise you feel would be an improvement. Please compare you answer with those of the author on page 205.

_____

_____

_____

_____

_____

_____

_____

_____

_____

_____

_____

_____

_____

6

Legal Instruments Of Transfer: The More You Know About Them The More Help You Can Be

A significant part of unfinished business is planning, preparing, and regularly reviewing a will or trust that describes how parents wish their estate to be distributed. Most senior family members gain considerable satisfaction from the preparation of these documents. Some require the help of their adult children to contact lawyers and get the process started.

- "After my son, a local attorney, and I struggled through the preparation of my will, I found peace of mind."

- "It's a great feeling for all family members when things are in order legally."

71

- "When my daughter and I got around to working with a lawyer on my will, we discovered it brought us closer together."

Those senior family members who need wills often fall into one of the following classifications:

The Delayers. These individuals dread the process so much that they either postpone it too long, or handle it in such a cursory way that it brings little or no satisfaction. They say, "It's such an ugly subject that I just can't get around to doing anything at this point. Besides, what's the hurry? Laws keep changing, and I'll have plenty of time later." These parents may be sending their adult children a signal that they want or need to be persuaded to take action.

The Worriers. These senior family members agonize over every detail of a will until they drive themselves, their families, and their lawyers to distraction. Then, once the will is complete, they continue to make frivolous or unnecessary changes. Adult children who have parents that are worriers may need to take a firm stand on getting a will completed, and then insure that "picky" changes are not constantly required.

The Realists. These parents accept the need for a will (or trust), and deal with it in an open forthright manner. When necessary, they do not hesitate to make changes. "I feel good that our will is made, but we still have to be realistic and change it now and them. Every time there is a situation like a divorce, we are forced to rethink the distribution of our estate." These parents often keep their adult children on edge, but they always know where things stand.

If your parent(s) have yet to make arrangements for the distribution of their estate, and are receptive to help, now may be the time to work in concert with them (and perhaps other family members) on a partnership or "team" basis. The more key family members know about the legal aspects of unfinished business, the more help they can be. For those who do not have experience with wills and trusts, the following pre-test is a good place to start.

PRETEST FOR ESTATE PLANNING

Check your responses with the answers provided to ensure any misunderstandings are immediately corrected. If wills and trusts are new to you, you may miss several questions. You may also surprise yourself with how much you already know.

True   *False*

_____   _____   1. Only the wealthy need wills.

_____   _____   2. A primary purpose of a will is to help you specify and delineate your bequests.

_____   _____   3. "Intestate" is the legal phrase for dying without a will. It means the state will process your estate according to its laws.

_____   _____   4. Once you have a will, nothing you own can pass to a person outside it.

_____   _____   5. A holographic (hand-written) will does not require witnesses.

_____   _____   6. In a joint-tenancy arrangement, one party automatically becomes sole owner upon the death of the other party.

_____   _____   7. A no-risk approach to preparing a will is to buy a standard form from a stationery store and fill it out yourself.

_____   _____   8. If you have an attorney draw up your will, it's a good idea to settle on the fee at the first meeting. For existing clients, attorneys usually do wills at a nominal sum.

_____   _____   9. If one is older and has $250,000 in his or her estate, it would be foolish to investigate a trust.

_____   _____   10. To the courts a "common disaster" means one spouse dies ahead of the other.

_____   _____   11. A trust is a legal document by which you transfer assets such as money or real estate to a trustee to manage for any beneficiary or beneficiaries named.

_____   _____   12. A testamentary trust is considered part of your will and will pass through probate.

PRETEST FOR ESTATE PLANNING (cont.)

True   *False*

_____   _____   13. One potential of a trust is to provide money to a beneficiary in small amounts so they will not make foolish spending mistakes and use their part of the estate too quickly.

_____   _____   14. The executor and trustees are one and the same.

_____   _____   15. You cannot change an irrevocable trust.

_____   _____   16. It is always best to have a friend as an executor or trustee because they know your wishes better than a professional.

_____   _____   17. A codicil is the style of handwriting you use to sign your name to a will.

_____   _____   18. Under the new laws, there are no tax advantages to the preparation of a trust.

_____   _____   19. An executor's job is finished once an estate is settled.

_____   _____   20. A trust is never part of a will.

Total Correct _____

Answers: (1) F (a will is equally important in the settlement of any estate); (2) T; (3) T (this you want to avoid); (4) F; (5) T (there are many ways you can do this legally); (6) T; (7) F (it's wise to work with an attorney, and their fees for preparing wills are usually very reasonable); (8) T (don't be afraid to ask — it's a good idea); (9) F (anyone with a sizable estate might benefit from looking into trusts); (10) F (a common disaster is when both spouses die at the same time); (11) T; (12) T; (13) T; (14) F (you'll discover the difference in the chapter); (15) T; (16) F (selecting an executor or a trustee is a personal choice; sometimes it's better to have a professional, but a fee would be involved); (17) F (a codicil is a legal addition to a will); (18) F (there are still many tax advantages); (19) T; (20) F (although independent, it is still part of the will).

BE FAMILIAR WITH NAMES OF ASSET OWNERSHIP

Soon you will have an opportunity to prepare a form that can assist your lawyer in estate planning. Completing this form in advance can save money if your lawyer charges by the hour. Filling it out will also demonstrate your family is "in charge." This may result in your receiving better attention, and perhaps, a more thoughtful will. For example, knowing the form of assets' ownership will show you are knowledgeable. Some of the most common forms of asset ownership are:

- **Tenancy in common:** When a person along with other tenants (owners) in a given asset have certain, not necessarily equal, shares. The share owned constitutes part of the estate, and it may be disposed of in a will.

- **Community property:** This is an asset of a marital relationship in some, but not all states. When an asset is held in this manner, you can dispose of only your share (50 percent) through a will. Once listed as community property, a change to another form of ownership will require a mutual decision. At a first meeting with a lawyer, he/she may suggest you change from the community property to the joint tenancy form of ownership for the reasons explained below.

- **Joint tenancy:** A joint-tenancy ownership allows one party automatically to become sole owner of an asset upon the death of the other party. When one party or joint tenant dies, assets do not pass through a will.

You will discover additional information about forms of ownership and their advantages and disadvantages when you meet with a lawyer.

KNOW THE NAME OF A POSSIBLE TRUSTEE AND EXECUTOR IN ADVANCE

A trustee and executor are individuals that are designated to see that a will is carried out. In some cases, this person may be asked to manage property. A trustee and executor can be the same person. You and your parent should discuss this matter and make tentative selections before meeting with a lawyer.

A trustee or executor can be:

- An adult child
- Another family member
- A friend
- A professional (attorney, accountant)
- A trust department in a bank

With this brief background, you are now ready to participate (with a parent or perhaps other key family member) in the completion of the following preconsultation form. It will probably mean digging out important documents and policies, but this is part of unfinished business. Once the form has been completed, those involved can anticipate a more productive meeting with an attorney. Thanks to some advanced planning on your part, the basic homework has been accomplished.

PRECONSULTATION FORM

This form is to be completed by those preparing or updating their wills before the first appointment with a lawyer. Do it in pencil so changes can be made easily.

1. Carefully list all assets and additional information as indicated.

Asset*	Value	Date Acquired	Marital Status at Time	Form of Ownership

2. List the names of intended beneficiaries and other data. For tax purposes, it is important for your attorney to know the line of succession between you and your beneficiaries. Normally, but not always, people list their lineal descendants in order and then add others. Your attorney's advice will be significant here.

Benficiary	Relationship	Amount of Money or % of Estate	Specific Assets*

*You may list separate pieces of property, specific jewelry, automobiles, or any tangible asset you may have. Your lawyer may suggest this be consolidated on a separate list outside the actual will. If you do this, keep in mind that specific bequests are not only difficult to list but also subject to whimsical changes that annoy attorneys. Give your list careful thought to avoid unnecessary changes. Many people simplify their lists by giving things away ahead of time.

PRECONSULTATION FORM (cont.)

3. Alternative distribution in case both parents are killed in a common disaster or something happens to a primary beneficiary. This is optional but a good idea to plan for in the unlikely event it might happen.

Beneficiary	Relationship	Amount of Money or % of Estate	Specific Assets

4. After careful investigation, list the names of your executor and alternate in the spaces below:

Executor: _____
(Name)

_____
(Address)

_____
(Telephone)

Alternate
Executor: _____
(Name)

_____
(Address)

_____
(Telephone)

Congratulations! You are now ready to make an appointment with the lawyer you and your parent(s) choose. This meeting should be viewed as an enjoyable, educational experience. (As an adult child, you may or may not have prepared your own will.) Keep in mind the Mutual Reward Theory applies to all relationships — even those of a professional nature. Once all parties are satisfied with the will, progress has been made. Keep it in a safe place (home file, safe, or bank safe deposit box) where you and the senior family member can get to it easily and quickly in case of an emergency or when changes are necessary. If your parents wish to establish an atmosphere of openness, copies of the will can be provided to all siblings. A signed copy is as good as an original will.

KEEPING A WILL UPDATED

For a few, it is now possible for people, in concert with their attorneys, to maintain wills on a home computer. This makes them easily changeable and provides other advantages. Even though a computerized will is not presently realistic for most, your will should be viewed as an ongoing document and not a once-in-a-lifetime creation forever sealed and stored in a secret place. Wills need to be updated every so often because of such possibilities as:

- A change of mind;

- A recent inheritance or assets not covered in a previous will;

- A marriage, birth, adoption, divorce, or death may dictate a revision;

- Or new laws that may mandate changes.

PROTECTING YOUR ESTATE FROM UNNECESSARY TAXES

Your parents have worked hard to accumulate their estate, and they will want to pass as much of it as possible on to you and other family members. Protecting an estate from excessive taxes normally moves on into a higher level of money management. Often, this requires the advice of professionals such as tax specialists, lawyers, financial planners and/or trust officers. To avoid extra expenses, your parent and you may want to go directly to an attorney.

People involved in sizable estates should attend classes and read articles that discuss whether one may or may not wish to avoid probate. The more you and your loved one can learn about legal options to avoid probate, the better. Be careful, however, because estate-tax planning is complex. Your best decision may be to find the right professional. This person should know current federal and state estate tax laws as well as recent applicable court cases. The right person will help develop a plan that both takes advantage of tax provisions and accomplishes the wishes of the senior family members.

SETTING UP A TRUST

A trust is a way to leave money that can take advantage of tax benefits, and accomplish the desires of the person setting up the trust. Trusts can be arranged both before a person dies or to take effect upon his or her death. In a trust, part or all of an estate is assigned to a trustee or trustees to manage and distribute in the manner prescribed. It is a way to control the release of money either before or after death. Trusts bring peace of mind because things are prearranged by the aging parent. Naturally, if one family member assumes the responsibility of helping prepare either a will or a trust, this person should share the results openly with others and not arrange matters in his or her favor.

Mrs. K's Solution

Mrs. K's later years were made beautiful by her granddaughter, Ruth, who took time to know and enjoy her only grandmother. Mrs. K loved her daughter, Ruth's mother, but did not want her to be in charge because she had been married three times and never demonstrated she could manage money. Mrs. K's answer: A trust arrangement would provide Ruth a sum of money each month until she was 25 years of age, at which time she would receive the balance in a lump sum.

Mr and Mrs. Graber

Mr. and Mrs. Graber have four children. All are self-sufficient except Myrt, who was retarded at birth and has required special care all her life. How could Myrt be cared for best? Answer: a special trust arrangement. The other children were a part of the trust, and they were consulted about the special provisions for Myrt.

Mrs. Jackson

Mrs. Jackson could not have been happier with her 12 grandchildren. She spent much of her time traveling to see them. They were the center of her life for more than 15 years. What might she do to help them later? Answer: a trust that would equally distribute Mrs. Jackson's estate among all 12 grandchildren when each reached a certain age. The details were worked out with a lawyer and administered by a trust officer in a local bank. An annual fee was charged for this service.

TESTAMENTARY VERSUS LIVING TRUSTS

A testamentary trust is a separate legal document incorporated in a will. A person designates the purpose and specifics in his or her will and also designates a trustee. When the person dies, the testamentary trust goes into effect.

A so-called living trust is not a specific part of a will. A living trust can be designed to end after a specified period of time before or after one's death. A living trust can be either revocable or irrevocable. If revocable, a person retains the right to change the terms of the trust, or even end it, during his or her lifetime. In other words, the creator of the trust remains in charge. If your parent(s) establish an irrevocable trust, then he and/or she cannot ordinarily change the terms or end it. Though inflexible, an irrevocable trust does offer special tax advantages which can be explained by a professional.

STRUCTURE VERSUS FLEXIBILITY IN A TRUST

The basic problem in setting up any trust is the uncertainty of what will happen in the future. It is possible to spend hours developing an arrangement that does not ultimately accomplish one's desires because of some unanticipated change. On the other hand, if one simply leaves an estate to beneficiaries hoping they will spend the money according to one's wishes, it might not happen that way either.

Many seniors like trusts because it is possible to make a more direct contribution to their grandchildren. It is not that they mistrust their children; they simply feel better knowing provisions are made for grandchildren in the event of a divorce or if their children are unsuccessful in building estates of their own.

Once again, the more advance thinking, the better prepared you and a parent will be when you consult a lawyer. Spouses and children need to discuss things ahead of time to avoid arguments in the presence of their attorney. No one, including your lawyer, should do the thinking for a capable senior.

NAMING A TRUSTEE

Selecting a trustee involves many of the same considerations as selecting an executor. However, there is a difference between the two. An executor's job is to see that the specific provisions of the will are followed. This usually happens within a year or two. A trustee manages a trust (makes investments, etc.) and sees that disbursements are made. A trust can continue for many years.

A parent can choose a child, personal friend, a relative, a professional, or the trust department of an institution as trustee. There are advantages and disadvantages to each. A personal friend or child may know and understand a parent and the beneficiaries, but may not be experienced with investments. A professional may not know beneficiaries but has the experience. A trust department in a bank won't move away or die. It also has a staff of professionals. Finally, the cost of a trust must be taken into consideration.

If you name a personal acquaintance or relative as trustee of a living trust, the fee will be whatever is agreed upon — often no fee at all. Professional trustees, however, receive fees that are either a set amount or a percent of the trust's assets. Fees should be discussed and negotiated ahead of time.

LETTER OF INSTRUCTION

Once you have completed your will and trust arrangements have been completed, you and your parent will probably want to prepare a letter of instruction for beneficiaries. This letter is a guide to make it easier for family to close out affairs. Although not a legal document, it should be in agreement with the terms of the will. You or your parent may want to check with your attorney on this matter. This letter of instruction may be written or placed on audio or video tape. Most people write a letter.

Instructions on how to complete a Letter of Instruction for personal property will be covered in detail later in this book.

APPOINTING A CONSERVATOR FOR AN ELDERLY PARENT

What can a caring adult child who lives in New York do if she or he has a parent in Los Angles who is no longer able to cope? A possible solution would be to find and appoint a local conservator or professional guardian. A conservator has to be appointed by the court and requires a lawyer. The individual appointed may or may not be a lawyer.

A *conservator* is an individual who assumes responsibility for seeing that a person receives the best possible care available within the budget allowed. Such a person is a protector, arranger, or guardian — not a care-taker. A conservator, for example, might handle business matters an adult child would normally take care of if she or he lived closer. This could include taking over assets and helping a lawyer in the preparation of a will or trust for your approval.

In some large communities, it is possible to hire private professional guardians. For those lacking funds, a court can appoint a conservator. When a public conservator is appointed, a review is required by the court to ensure a degree of accountability. In private situations, it is always a good idea to have the conservator bonded. Conservators are not licensed, so careful investigation and caution should be used.

INSURANCE CONSIDERATIONS
(A Team Approach)

Senior family members often become unnecessarily emotional about insurance decisions. This is natural, especially when insurance coverage is viewed as a security blanket. The fear of being left unprotected and a family burden increases geometrically as one ages. As many politicians have learned the hard way, it is not wise to tinker with Social Security benefits.

Because of both real and exaggerated fears, the preparation and maintenance of the best possible insurance "protection package" should be a team effort which includes the senior family member and a person whose judgment is trusted (usually an adult child or other family guardian). The following is strongly recommended:

1. An annual review to determine if the best coverage based upon available funds is in place and premiums have been paid.

2. Nothing should be added to or cancelled in a policy without a second opinion.

3. The purchase of a new policy should have the approval of the senior, adult child, and a professional independent insurance agent.

Although all insurance policies or programs (life, automobile, homeowners, accident, pre-paid funeral expenses, etc.) should be reviewed, two programs deserve special consideration:

Medicare Supplements. As good as Medicare is, it does not take care of all medical expenses — and the gap continues to widen. Thus, some form of supplement is almost essential. A wide variety of programs are available (some better than others). To find the "best" one will take a good deal of research.

Institutional Care Programs. Perhaps the greatest fear of an aging individual is the thought of going to a care facility (nursing home). In most situations, when this becomes necessary and the aging individual has limited income and assets (under a prescribed level) the government will handle the cost. For others who have assets, insurance is a consideration. Normally, premiums are high, the coverage period short, and other limitations prevail. Therefore, no other insurance area should receive more scrutiny. Seniors and adult children should be "open" and forthright in discussing the options. Here again, a trusted insurance agent should be consulted.

Chapter 21 in *COMFORT ZONES: A PRACTICAL GUIDE TO RETIREMENT,* also written by the author of this book, is devoted exclusively to insurance matters. It is recommended as a guide to both seniors and adult children. Contact Crisp Publications, Inc., 95 First Street, Los Altos, California 94022 for more information.

Professional conservators normally charge between $40.00 and $70.00 per hour. They are available for emergencies, and because they know about local support groups, legal processes, and similar matters, they can be considered consultants.

As long as the aging individual can function without a conservator, she or he should be allowed to do so. A guardian is most needed when an aging person can no longer deal soundly with medical, monetary, and/or legal matters, thereby making that person vulnerable to abuse from others.

As is true in granting a power of attorney, appointing a conservator is potentially risky, and should be done only after a thorough investigation.

SUMMARY

1. A will or trust is a way to distribute an estate among beneficiaries which has tax advantages.

2. When aging parents do not complete wills or trusts on their own when they are fully capable of doing so, adult children may need to urge them and help with the process. Even when such instruments have been completed, adult children may need to assist if last minute changes become necessary.

3. When help is required, all key family members need to be involved or informed. The process can be a positive experience for all concerned.

FAMILY STUDY #11   **Mr. Monroe Upsets The Family**

Mrs. Monroe slipped away peacefully one night three months after she and her husband, Harry, had celebrated their 50th wedding anniversary. The shock to Harry was so great he fell into a two-year depression. During this period he moved from one family to another (there are two sons and two daughters, all with families of their own). Through family persuasion, Harry finally sold the old home and moved into an elegant retirement center where all levels of care and service are available. Harry was 82 when he moved into the center, and the entire family gave a sigh of relief.

Not long after moving in, one daughter, Sylvia, started receiving reports that her father had been seen in various places with another woman, somewhat younger, from the same retirement center. Subsequent news was that Mr. Monroe and his new friend had taken an extended cruise — something he had never done with their mother.

Sylvia immediately called a family meeting. With the four siblings and their spouses in attendance, Sylvia expressed her feelings by saying, "I think that Dad has gone overboard with this woman. From what I can gather, she can get him to do anything she wants. I'm fearful Dad will be taken in now and hung out to dry later. And, as you all know, Mom and Dad had a will splitting the estate evenly among all of us and our children. Under the state inheritance laws, everything has now passed to him, and Dad can change things anytime he wants without consulting us. I think we should consider stepping in now before Dad gets hurt and before the financial matters become so complicated that we all lose out. Besides. I have this feeling that once she gets what she wants, she will drop him like a hot potato."

Without any facts to go on, the family came up with five tentative options.

1. Have their Dad arrange for Sylvia to meet his friend;

2. Have their Dad arrange a family gathering for all family members to meet his friend;

3. Have a family meeting with Dad, introduce the subject, and ask what he plans for the future;

4. Tell Dad to take care of himself and his own happiness and not be concerned about inheritance possibilities;

5. Discuss with Dad how their mother's wishes (the distribution of the estate) might be accomplished.

What do you think of the options? What would you change or add? Write your opinions in the space below and compare your answer with suggestions on page 205.

FAMILY STUDY #12   Mom's Decision

In some respects, Dorothy has benefited from having her mother live with her. She has had less housework to do and consequently more time to devote to her career as a paralegal professional. Also, she has been free to take trips and enjoy a good social life. Fortunately, her mother has been both understanding and grateful. The relationship has been mutually rewarding.

Starting about six months ago, however, Dorothy noticed that her mother was having increasing trouble coping with things she handled well in the past. Then, last Sunday, she asked Dorothy to draw up her will based upon a formula that she had devised. With five other children in the family, her mother's estate, evenly divided, would amount, after legal costs and inheritance taxes, to about $50,000 per adult child. But, her mother was adamant in saying, "I want the other children to have around $10,000 each and you to have the rest. You deserve it and I won't feel right unless you receive it. I think the other children will understand, but if they don't, it is still the way I want it. Please work with one of the lawyers at your office and have the will prepared as soon as possible."

Dorothy is deeply troubled over the matter. She has always had good relationships with her brothers and sisters, and they have all appreciated Dorothy's contribution in caring for Mom. Still, some of them need money more than Dorothy, and she would feel more comfortable if the estate were divided equally.

What, in your opinion, should Dorothy do? Write out your answer and then compare with the views expressed on page 206.

_____

_____

_____

_____

_____

_____

_____

7

Respect Resistance and Encourage Replacements

"There is a paradox in pride: it makes some men ridiculous, but prevents others from becoming so."
Charles Caleb Colton (1780-1832)

To people in the workplace, R & R means Rest & Recreation — a recovery time before returning to the challenge. To those who have retired, R & R might mean Resistance & Replacement.

Too much rest after retirement can encourage a sedentary life that encourages aging. Resistance to inactivity is essential. And, as one reaches later years, previous levels of recreation must give way to substitutes. One must often be satisfied to walk or jog leisurely rather than running. Replacement is essential in order to prevent one from "giving up."

THE NATURE OF RESISTANCE

Resistance at any age can be interpreted positively because it may mean that one is demonstrating self-reliance and self-determination. So, in one sense, the more resistance an elderly person demonstrates the better. He or she is simply expressing a feeling of determination — the kind of "pioneer spirit" so often valued in our culture.

Senior family members have earned the "right to resist" changes that do not appeal to them. If giving up something important (like car or home) does not fit into their time schedule, they should put up a fight. If they wish to "show others" that they are still in charge, it can be a healthy response.

Resistance by seniors should therefore be considered normal and not stubborn behavior. It should be viewed as a positive factor, and not just inflexibility.

RESISTANCE AS A DETERRENT TO THE AGING PROCESS

Perhaps you know an older person who is tenaciously holding on to the right to live in his or her home. Is this resistance healthy? Or maybe you know an individual who, against the advice of family, continues to take camping trips into wilderness country. Will this determination slow the aging process? Or what about a resident in a nursing home who insists on making her own bed and walking (without help) to dinner each night. Should this kind of pride be encouraged as an anti-aging involvement?

Sometimes adult children discuss their aging parents without fully realizing what they are saying.

"My dad is a tough old bird who is increasingly impossible to deal with."

"My mother is stubborn beyond understanding. When I make a suggestion, she tells me she is capable of fighting her own battles — even if it is obvious she is not."

The message under the message in both comments is that both individuals are fighting the aging process with great courage. They may be difficult to deal with, and they may carry resistance too far, but it is their life they are trying to extend.

HEALTH ALERT

The most frequent fear of aging people is the deterioration of their health. Reinforcement by family members through positive comments are helpful.

"You should be proud of the way you are getting around these days."

"You are doing much better than Mary's mother and you are at least ten years older."

"I hope I can stay in good physical shape like you, Pop."

A big advantage to frequent parental visitations by adult children is the opportunity to receive first hand both verbal and visual signals that all is not well physically, or that a doctor should be consulted. Senior family members are often masters at hiding serious ailments.

A change in medicine can sometimes cause side effects not anticipated by doctors. Whenever you or an aging person you care about changes drugs (or the amount taken), close monitoring is suggested. If an abnormal reaction occurs, a doctor should be consulted immediately.

Should an aging individual appear confused while taking prescribed drugs, the person's doctor should be consulted, and corrective action should be taken. Sometimes written reminders or a pill box is all that is needed. In more serious situations, other controls may be necessary.

While concern is natural, over-concern and excessive queries by an adult child about the health of an aging parent can be counter-productive.

RESISTANCE VS. DETERMINATION

Resistance should not be confused with determination. Many elderly parents are determined to live their lives and make the most of things — they are not trying to be obstreperous. Many are fighting an inner battle for survival that often spills over into what can be interpreted as difficult behavior. When stubbornness to "live life their way" does not interfere with normal self-care, it should be encouraged by adult children. Of course, knowing this does not always make it easier for adult children, but it can help. Anyone who is willing to fight the aging process deserves respect, and respect can increase the understanding of the support person.

PRIDE AS A BARRIER TO ACCEPTING LOWER EXPECTATIONS

You may have heard expressions similar to these from elderly people: "When I can no longer play 18 holes of golf on a regulation course, I will give up the game." "If I can't continue to play bridge without making embarrassing mistakes, then it is time to call it quits." "When I am no longer able to go out in public without others wanting to help me with every step, it is time to stay home."

It if difficult for proud people to accept substitutes that are below their personal expectations or previous standards. Some seniors would rather not travel at all, if they have to do so at a moderate pace; or rather not go out to dinner if they must be so careful about what they eat or drink that the "fun" is gone. For those with excessive pride, half a loaf is not better than nothing at all. Many would rather stay home and become television addicts. Herein lies the problem. Rather than accept substitutes, some "give up," and as a result, often encourage their "aging process."

PICK AND CHOOSE

The remainder of this chapter consists of four exercises. The name and purpose of each is listed below. It is suggested that the reader become familiar with all four so that they can be utilized when the need arises.

1.   **KITTY EXERCISE:** This is designed to make it easier for seniors to spend money more freely on little things that will enhance their lives.

2.   **REPLACEMENT EXERCISE:** This will give adult children and other caretakers tips on replacement of activities aging individuals can no longer continue. Some examples are provided.

3.   **CONVERSION TABLE:** This exercise makes suggestions on converting a high energy activity into a more comfortable one or safer approach. Ask the senior family member to read this first and then discuss it.

4.   **RESISTANCE EXERCISE:** This presents techniques that will help an adult child overcome stubborn resistance from a parent when such resistance is not in her or his best interests. This can prove to be most helpful when the time is right.

KITTY EXERCISE

Many of today's seniors were heavily influenced by the austerity of the depression years. As a result, they often find it difficult (some say "like pulling teeth"), to pay for taxi rides, long distance telephone calls, or other modest expenditures that would enhance their lives. Their earlier experiences cause them to view modern prices as wasteful or ridiculous. They do not sense that such "saving" can be destructive to their physical or mental health. Such attitudes often have no relation to wealth.

This simple exercise is designed to help parsimonious seniors overcome this handicap in order to make their lives richer and help them to stay in charge longer.

An adult child whose mother has recently given up driving, might initiate a "taxi kitty" to encourage her mother to continue visiting friends and "circulating." The adult child (or other family member or friend) might start the kitty by donating an amount each month ($10 or $20) or encouraging the senior to form her or his own kitty with available funds.

It doesn't matter who contributes, the idea is to make it easier for seniors to spend money more freely for their own good.

Some possible "kitty pools" are listed below. Check those that you feel might enhance the life of a senior you may be assisting.

☐ **TAXI POOL**
(Explained above.)

☐ **TELEPHONE KITTY**
(Some adult children give their parents calendars with money attached to each month to encourage telephone calls to themselves or others.)

☐ **TIPPING POOL**
(This might help a few seniors to tip more freely and receive better service; also might encourage a few to eat out more often.)

☐ **STAMP KITTY**
(Instead of money, put stamps in this pool.)

☐ **EATING-OUT POOL**
(Senior parents benefit from the socialization that takes place during a luncheon or dinner party.)

☐ **TRAVEL KITTY**
(If necessary, different members of the family can contribute.)

☐ **HOUSEKEEPING/CLEANING POOL**
(It is healthy for the senior to contribute when it is possible.)

☐ **DRY CLEANING/LAUNDRY POOL**
(Seniors often delay such expenditures because they feel prices are excessive.)

☐ **OTHER KITTYS**
(List any other "kitty ideas" of your own, like a special shopping kitty for a specific purpose.)

| REPLACEMENT EXERCISE | It is a recognized policy among those who deal professionally with seniors to never take away an activity they can do for themselves. When it becomes necessary to discontinue certain activities, a search should be make for the best replacement. Listed below are some "substitute" examples. Check those you would use under similar circumstances. |

1. Mrs. Grant, age 81, is a highly independent widow. Two months ago she gave up driving and sold her car following a ticket she received for failing to honor a stop sign, and which almost resulted in a serious accident.

   Her daughter, seeing that her mother was beginning to retreat from social and community contacts, listed the following possible replacements:

   ☐ Initiate a "taxi kitty" so her mother would not worry about paying taxi fare to an important activity.

   ☐ Obtain a bus schedule and accompany her mother on a few trips until her mother volunteered to continue on her own.

   ☐ Arrange to drive her mother to professional or social appointments once a week.

   ☐ Offer to pay a driver for specific trips each month.

2. Mr. Page has "survived" the last ten years of his retirement mainly as the result of playing golf. Not only has it provided exercise, but also needed social involvement. Last fall Mr. Page (now 83) quit golf for two reasons: (1) the foursome he previously played with disbanded because two members passed away; (2) his eyesight has failed to the point he became frustrated and couldn't meet his previous high standards of play. Knowing this, Mr. Pages's son, John, listed the following substitutes that he might activate:

   ☐ Continue walking the course with his golf buddies.

☐ John would walk with his father more often.

☐ Purchase his father a new pair of walking shoes and a pedometer for his belt to measure distance walked.

☐ Convince his father to join a "walking club."

☐ Compliment his father frequently on his ability to stay thin and in good shape.

☐ Offer to pay the dues of a local health club that welcomes senior members and has a swimming pool.

3. After breaking her hip for the second time, Mrs. James was advised by her doctors to use a "walker" both in and out of her home. The big adjustment was attending church, almost one mile away, When Mrs. James's daughter learned that her mother was going to give up her church activities in favor of a religious television program, she listed the following steps she might take.

☐ Encourage her mother to contact a friendly neighbor (both members of the same church) to drive her to church services and other activities.

☐ Contact the church about what help they might provide.

☐ Contact her mother's neighbor and offer to pay her for gas or other expenses if she would drive her mother to church.

☐ If the neighbor becomes involved, take her and her mother out to lunch once a week to encourage the arrangement and relationship.

Reviewing this exercise suggests it is possible that the substitutes offered might keep Mrs. Grant involved in her community; Mr. Page active physically despite dropping golf; and Mrs. James involved in her church. All such substitutes can be an excellent deterrent to aging.

| CONVERSION EXERCISE | The longer a senior family member is able to continue primary activity, the better. A replacement is also better than giving up altogether. The idea is to stay as active as possible through prudent shifts to less demanding activities. Circle those replacements (adjustments) you have already made; place a checkmark in front of those replacements you might consider in the future. |

Sports

Activity	Replacement
18 holes of golf	9 holes of golf
singles tennis	doubles tennis
bicycling	exercycle
backpacking	walking
swimming 40 laps	swimming 20 laps
running	jogging or walking
night driving	take a bus or taxi

Social

square dancing	waltzing
independent travel	traveling with a tour group
evening bridge group	afternoon bridge group
leading church work	participating in church work
independent R.V. travel	group bus trips
department store shopping	catalog shopping

Home

enjoying big meals	enjoying small meals
having big parties	having small parties
evening meal out	luncheon meal out
drinking liquor	drinking wine or soft drinks
taking a bath	taking a shower
driving yourself	taking taxi/bus or senior transportation
walking unassisted	using a cane
using a cane	using a walker or wheel chair
having a large garden	being happy with a small garden or growing flowers inside.

Excessive pride often causes some aging parents to refuse replacements that would contribute to their health and lifestyle. Accepting losses is never easy, but it shows style to do so.

RESISTANCE EXERCISE

Assume that you are faced with a situation where you must overcome the resistance of someone you love for their own benefit, and your action is to minimize resistance, and at the same time, maintain the best possible relationship with the individual. Please read the list and check suggestions that you would accept and follow.

☐ Discuss with elder.

☐ Gain the full support of all family members to take a given action step.

☐ Have a (medical) professional by your side when the change is discussed so that the senior family member senses how serious the matter has become.

☐ Have a professional discuss the matter above with your parent (this could be a doctor, minister, or care expert).

☐ Discuss the situation only when you have another family member with you.

☐ Explain how a similar situation involving another aging individual was handled and how the senior benefited.

☐ Discuss a "plan" and ask your parent to consider it (i.e., "sleep on it") before making a decision.

☐ Simply present a "plan," state that "it is your life," and walk away hoping the individual will have accepted it when you return.

☐ Provide and encourage a suitable substitute.

☐ Write out all of the advantages and disadvantages in an attempt to get the senior family member to make a logical, rational decision.

☐ Use the "if you were in my place technique." That is, say, "This is for your own good. If you resist it, you will only hurt yourself."

Other: _____

_____

_____

_____

_____

THE GIFT OF ENCOURAGEMENT

There are many things others can do to enhance the lives of seniors, but providing encouragement to stay active and involved should receive top priority. Here's why.

As we move into our later years, we often develop what could be called the "doubt syndrome." For example, we might decide to take a trip, attend a social event, or try a new adventure and then suffer the agony of doubt to the point we cancel. In earlier years, we would have moved ahead with excitement and personal confidence. The "doubts" would not have surfaced.

Why does it happen?

Perhaps it is because risk-taking is simply more threatening. We somehow permit ourselves to settle into comfort zones where we feel safe, secure, and life is predictable. Any movement out of such zones seems unreasonably dangerous. Possibly it is a special kind of "senior fear" that emerges even though logic should tell us that with full lives behind us and less time ahead our fears should diminish because we have less to lose.

Whatever the cause, we need to have our confidence restored by those who care about us. We need to hear such expressions as, "you made the right decision," and "'You can do it,' over and over. Without this gift of encouragement, we may back away from taking reasonable risks too soon, and in so doing speed up our own aging process.

SUMMARY

1. Resistance to inevitable changes is normal at any age, especially as abilities diminish among seniors. When such resistance translates into greater personal determination, to "hang in there," such action may slow down the aging process.

2. As painful as it may be, accepting lower expectations in various activities is part of growing older.

3. One way to deal with resistance in an aging parent is to help them see the value of substitutes. Those who refuse to accept substitutes may speed up the aging process in themselves.

FAMILY STUDY #13   **What is the Answer?**

Mr. James, age 80, is an excellent example of a person who accepts the aging process gracefully and in stride. Dearly loved by family members, he has mellowed in recent years and is currently detached from much of the reality that surrounds him. Although Mr. James takes frequent walks and watches his diet carefully, he no longer fights for his independence, values, and beliefs. Mr. James frequently comments, "It is foolish to fight the inevitable and create your own stress. I intend to relax and enjoy these special years."

Mr. Wood, also 80, is a highly independent, somewhat cantankerous, individual who fights to remain independent and protect his identity. Mr. Wood follows an exercise and diet regime similar to that of Mr. James, but he refuses to mellow and accept the reality around him without a fight. As a result, he is often avoided by others, including members of his own family. Mr. Wood makes this comment: "The moment I give up fighting for what I believe in is the moment I will start to fall apart. Exercise and diet are important, but it is sheer determination to stay involved that slows the aging process. I may not be popular because of my feisty attitude, but I may be around longer because of it."

Do you agree more with Mr. James than Mr. Wood? Or is it the other way around? State your position in the spaces provided and then turn to page 206 to compare your answer with that of the author.

_____

_____

_____

_____

_____

_____

_____

FAMILY STUDY 14　　**Barbara Takes Over**

Barbara is almost a daily visitor a the nursing home where her father lives. A community leader and outstanding manager, Barbara frequently takes problems to the administrator, and as a result, her father receives favored treatment. For example, he has one of the best located rooms and more personal belongings than his roommate. He also receives excellent attention from the staff. Barbara showers everyone with gifts. She also constantly "monitors" the care of her father.

As a "take charge" person, Barbara takes care of all of her father's financial matters; correspondence to other family members (including grandchildren); and generally keeps her father immune from problems. Barbara feels this is the least she can do for her father who has provided love, encouragement, and financial support to her from infancy. She feels strongly that her father deserves the peace, quiet, and contentment that comes when others assume responsibility.

That is why Barbara was shocked this morning when her father said, "I'm tired of all of your over-protection. Let me fight my own battles in this place. Let me have some control over things outside. Just because my physical condition forces me to be here is no reason I should be smothered."

Is Barbara giving her father too much support? If her father fights his own battles inside the nursing home, will the reaction of staff be negative and reduce the level of care he receives? Write out your views and compare them with those on page 206.

_____

_____

_____

_____

_____

_____

_____

8

Community Support; Knowing What Is Available

"If a free society cannot help the many who are poor, it cannot save the few who are rich."
John F. Kennedy

It stands to reason that the more family members discover and utilize community support systems, the less they will need to do themselves. A combination of family and community support working together offers great promise. Thus, anyone starting to assume the challenge of helping a parent through the "unfinished years" needs to become familiar with available support systems within a given community, and when appropriate, see that they are utilized.

This does not mean that everything can simply be turned over to support groups while the adult child walks away. In the final analysis the adult child (or other family member) is in charge and needs to supervise the process.

Study the support pyramid illustrated below. As you do this, keep in mind that even though a religious organization is at the top of the pyramid (because it is often a key support group), the final support usually filters down to the family, which constitutes the foundation of the entire support system.

SUPPORT PYRAMID   The purpose of this diagram is threefold: (1) to show the importance of all support groups, both social and functional; (2) to demonstrate that the more support groups one develops, the longer "last stage" family support can be delayed; (3) to point out that support systems constitute a "bank of options." Sometimes one is more important than another but all are vital in a comprehensive plan.

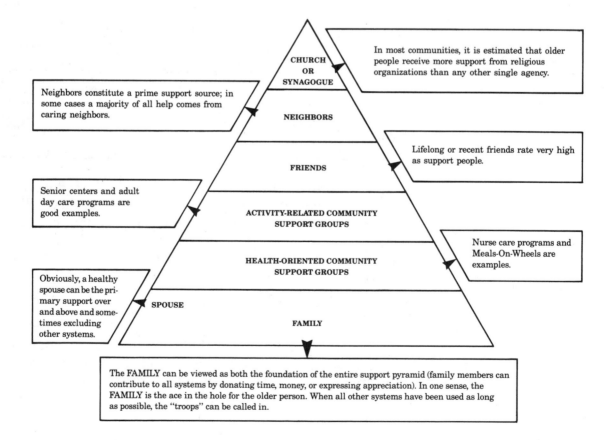

In most communities, it is estimated that older people receive more support from religious organizations than any other single agency.

Neighbors constitute a prime support source; in some cases a majority of all help comes from caring neighbors.

Lifelong or recent friends rate very high as support people.

Senior centers and adult day care programs are good examples.

Nurse care programs and Meals-On-Wheels are examples.

Obviously, a healthy spouse can be the primary support over and above and sometimes excluding other systems.

CHURCH OR SYNAGOGUE

NEIGHBORS

FRIENDS

ACTIVITY-RELATED COMMUNITY SUPPORT GROUPS

HEALTH-ORIENTED COMMUNITY SUPPORT GROUPS

SPOUSE

FAMILY

The FAMILY can be viewed as both the foundation of the entire support pyramid (family members can contribute to all systems by donating time, money, or expressing appreciation). In one sense, the FAMILY is the ace in the hole for the older person. When all other systems have been used as long as possible, the "troops" can be called in.

THE RIGHT COMBINATION Finding the right combination of family and community support, requires some research. Which agencies exist locally? What is their function? How do they receive their support? Which fit the future needs of senior family members and how might such community agencies be balanced with family support?

Community support systems are either private or government funded agencies organized to provide support for those who may not have family support systems, or in cases where the family support needs to be supplemented.

Community support agencies come in all sizes and forms. An agency might be strong in one community and weak or nonexistent in another. One might be a national agency, another could be local. Some are special, some provide functional assistance, some cover a wide range of services. View a neighbor or friend as a support person.

The number of different support organizations available depends on community size and government funding. Urban areas often have many separate services. Senior Centers often provide an amazing number of services, all from one location.

GAINING A NATIONAL PERSPECTIVE On the following pages, you will find sample lists of available support agencies. The list demonstrates the ranges of services available.

When It Comes To Locating Support Organizations —

SEEK

AND

YOU SHALL

FIND

The next few pages contain names, addresses or examples of where help can be found. This is by no means an exhaustive list, but provides some excellent resources which can, in turn, lead to to other sources of information and help.

NATIONAL LIST
NATIONAL SUPPORT ORGANIZATIONS
(Partial List)

Alzheimer's Disease and Related Disorders Association
70 E. Lake Suite 600
Chicago, Illinois 60601

Alzheimer's Disease International
360 N. Michigan Ave.
Chicago, Illinois 60601

American Association of Retired Persons
1909 K Street, N.W.
Washington, DC 20049
(202) 872-4700

American Geriatrics Society, Inc.
10 Columbus Circle
New York, NY 10019
(212) 582-1333

American Society on Aging
833 Market Street
Suite 516
San Francisco, CA 94130
(415) 543-2617

Arthritis Foundation
1314 Spring Street
Atlanta, GA 30309
(408) 872-7100

Commission on Legal Problems of the Elderly
1800 M Street, N.W.
Washington, DC 20036
(202) 331-2297

Foundation For Hospice and Homecare
519 C Street, N.E.
Stanton Park
Washington, DC 20002
(202) 547-7424

Gerontological Society of America
1411 K Street, N.W.
Suite 300
Washington, DC 20005
(202) 393-1411

Legal Research and Services for the Elderly
925 15th Street, N.W.
Washington, DC 20005
(202) 347-8800

National Association of Area Agencies on Aging
600 Maryland Avenue, S.W.
Suite 208
Washington, DC 20024
(202) 484-7520

National Association of Meal Programs
604 W. North Avenue
Box 6959
Pittsburgh, PA 15212
(412) 231-1540

National Council on the Aging, Inc.
600 Maryland Avenue, S.W.
West Wing 100
Washington, DC 20024
(202) 479-1200

National Hospice Organization
1901 N. Fort Myer Drive
Suite 902
Arlington, VA 22209
(703) 243-5900

NATIONAL HOME CARE ASSOCIATIONS

American Hospital Association, Division of Ambulatory and Home Care Services, 840 N. Lake Shore Drive, Chicago, IL 60611, (312) 280-6000; *Council of Community Health Services,* National League of Nursing, 10 Columbus Circle, New York, NY 10019, (212) 582-1022; *Home Health Services and Staffing Association,* 2101 L Street, N.W., Washington, DC 20037, (202) 775-4707; *National Association of Home Care,* 205 C Street, N.E., Washington, DC 20002, (202) 547-7424; *National Homecaring Council,* 67 Irving Place, New York, NY 10003, (212) 674-4990

EXAMPLES OF AREA SUPPORT ORGANIZATIONS*
(Partial list — addresses and telephone numbers should be obtained locally.)

Area Agency on Aging
Responsible for effective use of Federal Older American Act funds. Operates information and referral services.

Senior Citizens Information and Referral Service
This office provides referrals to agencies and programs designed to assist senior citizens.

Senior Employment Coordination
For those 55 and older who want to re-enter the work force.

Senior Shared Housing
Matches seniors with other citizens for the benefit of both — other seniors and younger people.

Long Term Care Ombudsman Services
Information and referrals on facilities, support groups, etc.

County Health Care Agency/Mental Health
Mental health assessment; individual and group consultations.

County Hotline
Crisis intervention and "Good Neighbor" telephone reassurance program.

Day Care Centers
Supervised social activities and/or rehabilitation

Social Services Agency
Applications for general relief and food stamps; in-home supportive services.

Housing — Government Subsidized Programs
Rental assistance for low-income elderly 62 and over.

---

* Look under **Area Agency on Aging** in your local telephone directory. If necessary, call the community library or local Senior Services Center for assistance. Area or county agencies are usually supported financially by a combination of federal, state, and county funds.

EXAMPLES OF COMMUNITY SUPPORT ORGANIZATIONS*
(Partial List — Addresses and Telephone Numbers Not Included)

American Association of Retired Persons

- Income tax assistance
- Crime prevention programs
- Supports nutritional programs
- Provides recreational programs

Adult Care Center

- For seniors who need rehabilitation
- Care for those suffering from Alzheimer's disease

Neighborhood House

- Offers food, clothing and information
- Visitations to elderly shut-ins

Senior Discount Program

- Discounts for people over 60 from participating merchants

Meals-on-Wheels

- Home-delivered meals once a day, five days a week to seniors who qualify. Delivered by volunteers. Modest charge.

Nutrition for Seniors Program

- Serves hot lunch Monday through Friday
- Recreational program

Phone Alert League (PAL)

- Offers a communications service to anyone living alone. If a client does not call PAL between a certain time, PAL will call and send someone to the home if necessary.

Counseling Service

- Professional counseling for social/mental problems. Fees: sliding scale according to ability to pay.

Postal Carrier Alert Program

- Postal carriers will report unusual or suspicious signs and relatives will be contacted

Department of Social Services

- Government agency
- In-home supportive services

Senior Information & Rental Service

- Information center for seniors; call for services other than those listed here

---

* Call your community library or Senior Services Center to see if they maintain a similar list to the one above. Also feel free to call local hospital discharge planners, United Way, churches and synagogues, or physicians. Consult your telephone directory and yellow pages under "Home Health Services" or "Nurses."

ATTITUDE TOWARD COMMUNITY SUPPORT SYSTEMS

When it is time to investigate which services are available in your community, the best approach is to let your fingers do the walking, and then "circulate." Start with a visit to a Senior Center, and make the rounds of all available agencies. Talk with those in charge. Read the available brochures. If there is a fee attached to a particular service, ask if Medicare (or other insurance) will take care of some or all of the expense. Make as many friends as possible and make a list of their names and telephone numbers. If possible, take the senior family member with you; or take a caring friend. Make an attempt to have the same attitude you would have if you were shopping for a special purchase. Nothing printed in this book can take the place of a personal investigation in your own community. Until you actually know what is available, you are operating in the dark!

PERSONAL PRIDE AND THE ACCEPTANCE OF COMMUNITY SERVICES

Unfortunately, some aging parents and their adult children delay investigating and accepting community services because of personal pride. This is like "cutting off your nose to spite your face," because:

- Some services are available only through a community agency.

- Many have professional staff members not found anywhere else.

- Many problems have been resolved because of early contact with a local agency.

- Some services are totally free.

- Volunteers are often dedicated seniors who are in a great position to communicate with the senior family member.

- If your community has an AARP chapter, it can not only provide you with many services but will give you personal contact with the largest most powerful association to help those over age 50.

- Often a senior family member who has been something of a recluse can find new "friends" who have volunteered at a local agency.

The expression "you can lead horses to water but you can't make them drink" may be applicable to the utilization of community services by many seniors. Friends and family members must locate and contact support groups for aging people, and then transport, accompany, and otherwise use their influence for a period of time until the aging individual feels comfortable.

> Mrs. Crane had to accompany her mother and participate in the activities herself before her mother started looking forward to the visits at the local Senior Center.
>
> John thought all he would have to do is deliver and pick up his father at the Adult Care Center. It turned out that John had to stay a few hours for the first three visits (playing checkers) before his father could make the adjustment.

When it comes to accepting what "seems good" for them, many seniors put up barriers based on legitimate fears and/or pride. In many cases, this should be anticipated. Often, if personal reassurance is provided for a few visits, the senior parent will not only adjust but start looking forward to the experiences.

TURNABOUT: SUPPORT GROUPS FOR ADULT CHILDREN

So far we have talked about support groups for seniors. If you are a member of the sandwich generation and have been frustrated in your attempts to assist an aging parent, what can you do? In many communities, there are support groups which help you to deal with senior family members. These groups consist of adult children who discuss the problems of aging, and provide reinforcement for each other. For example, adult children of those with Alzheimer's disease might find a local caretaker support group sponsored by A.D.R.D.A. (Alzheimer's Disease and Related Disorders Association).

HOSPICE
(A Special Support System)

The word Hospice was first used in medieval times to describe way-stations where religious orders gave medical and spiritual care to pilgrims journeying to and from the Holy Land.

Hospice is a philosophy of care that helps terminally ill patients and their families to gain control of their lives, while improving the quality of the dying person's remaining lifetime. One important purpose of Hospice is to provide terminally ill patients with the option of dying at home.

Concern for the total family is part of what makes Hospice care different from traditional forms of health care. Ideally, the terminally ill patient should be cared for at home by the family, and if appropriate, allowed to die there. Hospice teams assist the family not only in providing care but also in coping with the effects of the illness. Concern is for the physical, spiritual, psychological and social living of the terminal patient.

Referrals to the Hospice program can be made by the patient's private physician, the patient's family or the hospital discharge planner. Medicare now covers costs under the Hospice Program (agencies and hospitals running Hospice programs can provide details). For a patient to qualify for Medicare Hospice benefits, the patient's physician must certify that life expectancy is at a terminal state.

Check your telephone book under Hospice or call your local hospital for further details.

In addition to checking local sources (the same ones you would check for an aging parent), you might wish to write one or more of the following organizations:

CHILDREN OF AGING PARENTS — 2761 Trenton Road, Levittown, PA 19056

HAND IN HAND — 1909 K Street NW, Washington, DC 20049 (Model support group developed by AARP)

NATIONAL HOSPICE ORGANIZATION — 1901 N. Fort Myer Drive, Arlington, VA 22209 (Information on hospice care)

FAMILY SERVICE AMERICA — 44 East 23rd Street, New York, NY 10010 (May have a local agency that can provide counseling for adult children)

ALZHEIMER"S FAMILY SUPPORT GROUPS — U.S. F. Suncoast Gerontology Center, University of South Florida, P.O. Box 50, 12901 North 30th Street, Tampa, FL 33612

SENIORS HELPING SENIORS
(MRT at work)

With a growing population of retired persons, a longer lifespan due to medical advances, and a desire on the part of more seniors to remain active, it is only logical to anticipate that the opportunities for seniors to care for seniors will increase.

> Mrs. K (age 85) and Mrs. F (age 73) live in the same neighborhood. Mrs. K lives in a large home and is in good shape financially; Mrs. F rents a duplex and is having to skimp on food and other services in order to pay the rent that continues to increase. Mrs. K decided to employ Mrs. F as a live-in housekeeper and caregiver. The Mutual Reward Theory works because both parties come out ahead!
>
> Mr. J (age 86) lives in the same condominium complex with Mrs. S (age 71). At a modest monthly rate, Mrs. S spends three hours per day caring for Mr. J — she does much of the housekeeping, does all the shopping and takes him for rides, and spends a few hours each week writing Mr. J's correspondence. The money Mrs. S earns permits her to travel to Europe to visit relatives, attend local concerts, and maintain her independence. The Mutual Reward Theory is alive and well.

With wide variations, arrangements similar to those above are becoming more commonplace. Older people are taking care of older people. It appears to be a significant trend with advantages in all directions.

• Senior care-givers fight off the aging process by making a contribution while at the same time maintaining their independence.

• Older seniors receive companionship and care, and can often remain in their own living environments.

• Adult children can pursue careers and personal lifestyles with less pressure to care for their parents.

How might an older senior or adult child investigate such an arrangement? Here are four suggestions:

• Inquire around your neighborhood and among friends of senior members.

• Advertise in a local newspaper.

• Contact a local senior center.

• Contact local religious groups.

THE NEED FOR SUPPORT PEOPLE SHOULD NOT BE UNDERESTIMATED

When things are going well with a senior family member, the need to build relationships with support people in a community may appear to be a low-priority activity. The typical comment is, "We'll take care of things when the need arises." But, building support groups in advance can be almost as important as having good medical insurance. When the need becomes critical, knowing who to call can be important to both the aging parent and the adult child or friend.

The need for support of all kinds escalates geometrically during the final phases of unfinished business. It is then that we learn to appreciate those who care — supportive family members, friends, professional family counselors, clergy, and others. It is far easier to go through sadness, grief and sorrow when there are sensitive loving support people by your side.

Sadness starts when we sense that the person we care about is aging at an accelerated rate. It is a natural depressing state that is best accepted and discussed openly. When we lose a loved one, this sadness often turns to grief. Fortunately, with help of others, we usually work our way out of periods of sadness and grief without a residue of permanent sorrow or guilt. This is the most important contribution these support people can provide. Whenever a member of the clergy, a professional counselor, or friend intervenes or is invited to shepherd us through such difficult times, we are fortunate. With the right support, any guilt feelings can be minimized and sorrow on a permanent basis will not occur.

SUMMARY

1. Knowledgeable help is available in most communities. Often it is free or modestly priced.

2. Ignorance about what is available, apathy, or pride may keep aging family members and their adult children from taking advantage of these necessary services.

3. Adult children who make themselves aware of the available variety of community support services do their parents a favor. They also discover a range of support that will help them do a better job of unfinished business and ease the pressure on themselves.

ADVOCACY

As you become more involved in the problems of providing care for the elderly, you may wish to take a stand on significant issues in order to influence others — especially politicians. For example, in today's political climate, Congress acknowledges a national need for long-term care, yet is not willing to fund services currently being provided by families. They fully understand the demographic trends and realize the the numbers of people needing care will increase, while those available to provide caregiving in the home will decrease.

What is the answer? Some experts already believe that there are too many people in nursing homes simply because there is no family to provide the care they need at home. Do you agree? What can be done about it?

Advocates for change in the programs that currently serve the aging population need to demonstrate ways in which family caregiving can be expanded. It is either this, or more government involvement. Most caregivers are women. Many hold down full-time jobs. Should employers become more involved? Should voluntary caregivers be granted special tax advantages? What about including institutionalized care under Medicare?

There are many organizations through which you can make your preferences known. Two of the most important are:

American Association of Retired Persons
1909 K Street, SW
Washington, DC 20024

National Council on Aging, Inc.
600 Maryland Avenue, SW
Washington, CA 20024

FAMILY STUDY #15   Too Much Of A Good Thing

Ray is a patient loving husband and father. He calls himself a humanist because he always tries to give people precedence over other matters. Most of his friends refer to Ray as a "nice guy who will always listen."

For the last five years, Janice, Ray's wife, has been holding down a job, taking care of their three children, and devoting what time is left to her parents who live nearby. She visits her parents almost every day, does their shopping, washing, and many other things. Janice's giving does not bother Ray, although he sometimes feels that he is neglected because of her constant caring of her parents. What bothers him is that Janice's two sisters, who live in the same community, do little or nothing for their parents.

Yesterday, Ray took Janice out to dinner to talk the problem over and find a better solution. The evening turned into a bitter argument. It upset Ray so much he was unable to sleep. Janice, for some hidden reason, feels she needs to "make up" to her parents for the wonderful treatment she received as a child. She doesn't care what her two sisters do. When Ray stated that it was not fair for her to neglect him for her parents, she replied, "Ray, my parents will not be around as long as you and if you feel I am going overboard now, I'll make it up to you later."

If you were Ray, how would you approach the problem? Write out your answer below and compare it to the interpretation on page 207.

_____

_____

_____

_____

_____

_____

FAMILY STUDY #16   A Decision for the Parr Family

Nellie Parr and her brother, Randy, have contributed equally to the care and support of their arthritic mother, now 86 years of age, over the past five years. They have done a superb job both on a personal basis and by generating support from neighbors and friends. As a result, Mrs. Parr has remained safe and happy in her own home.

The problem now is that Mrs. Parr is becoming increasingly fragile and withdrawn. She doesn't even want her few remaining close friends to see her. She is not eating nutritious meals, her mobility is decreasing, housekeeping chores are neglected, and she is not bathing on a regular basis. Both Nellie and Randy are worried.

Together they have done some research. They know that in-home nursing care is available, housekeeping tasks can be done by another agency, and Meals On Wheels is available.

But, all of this help has been turned down by Mrs. Parr. She refuses to allow strangers into her home; she doesn't want neighbors to know she can no longer take care of herself. Her extreme modesty prevents her from letting another give her a bath. As Nellie says to Randy, "Our wonderful mother has too much old-fashioned pride for her own good. She hasn't said anything but maybe she wants one of us to invite her into our home. As we have discussed, it wouldn't work out in either of our busy homes. What can we do to convince her that accepting community help is the only way she can remain in her own home?"

Here are the options Randy and Nellie feel are open to them:

1. Suggest another alternative, like moving to a care facility, nursing home, or retirement center. Tell her it has to be one choice or the other.

2. Bring community support help into the home one at a time without gaining her full approval; start with Meals On Wheels, and then move into other support systems.

3. Set up a group meeting with the family minister and doctor present. Ask the minister to lead the meeting and the doctor to openly discuss the dangers of staying alone without some community support.

Which option do you prefer? Why?

_____

_____

_____

_____

_____

_____

_____

Compare your answers with those on page 208.

9

Support Strategies;
A Hypothetical Model
For Evaluation

"Nothing is more terrible than activity without insight."
Thomas Carlyle (1795-1881)

Sometimes an older person's health will take a quick turn for the worse, and an adult child will unthinkingly move in "to fix things and make them better." Sometimes this is done without a careful evaluation of the total situation and ongoing involvements.

When Jane's mother had a serious but temporary illness, Jane dropped everything and rushed to her mother's side to help. Two months later, after her mother had recovered, Jane was hospitalized from exhaustion. With a demanding husband, three teenagers, and a part-time job, Jane had over-extended herself. Not only did she injure her own health, but Jane's mother began to expect more help from her than she really needed.

119

Adult children often "rush" in to provide support without stopping to think about the long-term consequences. They do not consider the need for a strategy in which all siblings should help develop and execute. Although temporary emergency assistance is often necessary while a long-term strategy is being designed, overextending one's self and making needless mistakes during such periods can complicate instead of help matters. Obviously, a strategy prepared before an emergency need arises is the best plan of all.

In this chapter you will receive some tips and suggestions on how to devise a strategy to help aging parents remain in their own home as long as possible without endangering their health. Please complete the exercise that follows.

HOME CARE ASSISTANCE EXERCISE

This exercise is designed to give an adult child or friend as many specific suggestions as possible for enabling seniors to remain in their own homes. Some may be appropriate now, others later. Place a check mark in the square opposite any suggestion you feel is applicable and you would like to investigate further.

☐ Have the local gas company do a survey on the heating equipment and make energy-saving suggestions.

☐ Check into the availability of a daily/weekly visit from a professional "home care" service organization.

☐ Arrange for an electronic "beeper," which permits a senior living alone to call for assistance.

☐ Initiate a campaign to encourage other family members, neighbors, or friends to increase their visits.

☐ Arrange for a "meals-on-wheels" service (if appropriate).

☐ Check to see if there is a congregate meal site.

☐ Pay a neighbor (or other appropriate person) to check things on a daily basis.

☐ Have local police visit to see how the security of the home can be improved.

☐ If the senior has a terminal disease, investigate a Hospice program.

☐ For Alzheimer's patients, investigate the possibility of a local Day Care program to meet their special need.

☐ Construct a telephone "reassurance pal system."

☐ For aging people who spend too much time alone, look into the possibility of a Social Day Care program.

☐ Investigate a Day Health Care center, where physical therapy is possible.

☐ Look into the possibility of an organized Companion Care Program.

☐ Find out how you might arrange a Home Sharing plan; either a compatible older or compatible younger. Check with Senior Center or a local religious organization.

☐ Arrange for a bookkeeping, bill-paying service (if appropriate).

☐ Employ a visiting nurse.

☐ Consider the appointment of a public guardian.

☐ Find a "home care professional" to help you see that the home is safe from accidents — installation of rails, etc.

☐ Take this exercise to your local Senior Center and ask for additional ideas and suggestions.

Although not all adult children will take time to help design a long-term support strategy, those who do will discover many rewards.

DEFINING SUPPORT STRATEGY A support strategy is a "game plan" designed in advance to enhance the lives of elderly parents, and thus, conserve the amount of time, energy and money spent by adult children and/or close friend. It may start out providing a minimum of assistance (more should never be given than is really needed), but the plan should have provisions for accelerated support when required. Once in place, a strategy or goal can provide motivation and satisfaction to givers and recipients alike. Without a planned strategy, support will be provided on a haphazard basis. Elderly parents will not know what to expect; and adult children will not have the security and satisfaction of knowing a continuous system is in place and that their contribution is part of a total plan in which others are participating.

Those who become involved in developing a support strategy might benefit from asking themselves questions similar to these:

1. Does the strategy meet both the short and long-term needs of parent(s)?

2. Is the plan designed to encourage the highest level of involvement by the parent(s)?

3. Can the type and amount of support woven into the plan be provided on a consistent basis?

4. Is the plan financially feasible? Are funds available from parents, adult children, or government sources?

5. Does the strategy involve (to the degree they are able to participate) all siblings, other family members, and close friends?

6. Does the plan include some family "good times" to balance the work involved and improve relationships so that success possibilities of the plan are improved?

9. Is the strategy flexible? That is, if the parent(s) become stronger, can some phases of support be withdrawn until needed again? If additional support is needed quickly, does the plan make provisions to provide it?

10. Has the health and happiness (lifestyles) of participating adult children been taken into consideration?

Although each family should design a strategy to fit its own special and unique circumstances, the following hypothetical model (not intended to be perfect) is presented as a guide. The model illustrates a possible strategy for an "unfinished business" situation for one family only. It may be helpful to consider as a plan is formulated.

HYPOTHETICAL MODEL

The Situation

Mr. and Mrs. Johnson, both 85 years of age, live in a large older home in a community of 100,000 people. The Johnson's have four adult children. Christine is the oldest, Julia is next, and then John. Ray, the youngest, is considered the maverick and has distanced himself from the family circle.

Mr. Johnson requires daily medication because of a serious heart condition. Open-heart surgery has been ruled out by doctors because of his age and general health. Mr. Johnson has trouble walking. He often requires help from his wife in the bathroom.

Mrs. Johnson neglects her own needs to care for her husband. Dishes and clothes are often stacked, but left undone. Housework and repairs are neglected. Meals consist primarily of cereals, frozen dinners, or what family, friends, and neighbors might bring. Prescription drugs are not always taken on schedule. Because Mr. and Mrs. Johnson are proud and independent people (they refused to give up driving until last year), they find it difficult to ask for help.

The Johnson financial situation is marginal although there is no mortgage on the family home. Financial support from children or government sources may someday be necessary. There has been almost no communication among family members regarding financial matters.

Specific Strategy Agreements

Through preliminary meetings in the family home, Christine, Julia, and John, (and both parents much of the time), have devised an immediate strategy in which the three oldest will attempt to participate equally.

John volunteered to take over maintenance of the home, yard, and install safety devices throughout the home. John also said he would assist in paying bills and would consult in all other financial matter, including the establishment of a "support nest-egg" for future needs. John and his wife will work as a team, and will pay a personal visit each week.

Julia has agreed to help with the housework and washing. She will take her mother shopping when necessary. She will make two visits per week from her home 20 miles away. She is hopeful, however, that financial arrangements can be made for a part-time housekeeper.

Christine, who lives closer than John and Julia, volunteered to start out as the "leader" until a strategy was in place. She will be the "watchdog" to monitor the condition and progress of both parents, and if necessary, call an emergency meeting so that a group decision might be made. Christine said she would also act as a liaison with doctors and supervise the taking of prescribed medicines.

Christine and Julia have also volunteered to work together to discover the availability of community resources for both a short and long-term basis.

General Strategy Agreements

With considerable involvement by both Mr. and Mrs. Johnson, general agreement on several matters was reached. These included:

1. An "open door" policy will be maintained at future meetings. Spouses and grandchildren (a few already married) will be invited as will important support people such as neighbors or professionals.

2. Julia will increase communication with Ray so he will know what is going on, and be invited to participate in the future.

3. A "good time" period (usually around a family dinner), will follow each meeting.

4. Should pressure become too great on any family member, others will pick up the slack. It was recognized that Christine, Julia, and John's spouses deserve special consideration and equal support in the future, when their parents may require it.

5. Mrs. Johnson made the comment that knowing support is available is almost as good as receiving it. Everyone agreed to take time for as much communication as possible during individual visits and at "strategy meetings."

6. With agreement from Mr. and Mrs. Johnson, it was decided that the first part of the strategy would be one of exploration, preparation, as well as action. Future meetings would refine and update the preliminary plan.

First Strategy Review Meeting

John and his wife reported on the improvements they had made around the home. Julia and Christine complimented their parents for their independence, stating they seemed to be doing more for themselves. The surprise of the meeting was the extent of community support available and what had already taken place.

1. The Johnson's church is sending a visitor once a week, plus transportation for Mrs. Johnson to attend Sunday services.

2. A neighbor, Mrs. Valdez, is now on the alert to call Christine should she notice any changes. Christine, her mother, and Mrs. Valdez had lunch together last week.

3. Mrs. Jason, an old friend of the family, has volunteered to take both Mr. and Mrs. Johnson for a drive each week. Christine plans to take Mrs. Jason to lunch once a month.

4. Starting next week, Meals-on-Wheels will deliver hot meals each weekday at noon. Financial arrangements have been made.

5. Christine and Julia said they would continue to investigate local Home Care agencies for possible future use. They said that within a few months they could have a complete community support plan put together.

Just before the formal part of the meeting ended, everyone expressed satisfaction with the progress that had been made. Mr. Johnson, showing unexpected enthusiasm, suggested an agenda be made for the next meeting. He thought a review of their Will might be in order. Mrs. Johnson agreed. Christine said she would work up an informal agenda on other long-term matters. Helen, John's wife, volunteered to bring refreshments at the next gathering.

EVALUATION OF MODEL

Similar to a military or business strategy, a family plan to handle "unfinished business" needs (1) a starting point; (2) continuity; (3) flexibility to take care of future needs and changes; and (4) ongoing review. Based on the starting point and the first meeting, how would you rate the Johnson family strategy? Please use the evaluation form on the following page.

MODEL STRATEGY RATING FORM

	Yes	No	I Don't Know
1. Will the strategy adequately protect the lifestyles of adult children?	☐	☐	☐
2. Will the strategy eventually turn out to be mutually rewarding to all?	☐	☐	☐
3. Does the strategy include enough "good times" (birthday parties, anniversaries, traditional holiday gatherings) to sustain the plan?	☐	☐	☐
4. Is the strategy premature?	☐	☐	☐
5. Does the plan make good preliminary use of community resources?	☐	☐	☐
6. Is there a fair responsibility balance among siblings?	☐	☐	☐
7. Is there sufficient "leadership" to maintain the strategy?	☐	☐	☐
8. Does the plan provide enough provisions for accelerated care, if needed?	☐	☐	☐
9. Is the strategy realistic?	☐	☐	☐
10. Is there evidence of "over-planning?"	☐	☐	☐

HOW TO HELP AGING PARENT(S) MAINTAIN
THEIR OWN SUPPORT SYSTEM WHEN YOU ARE MILES AWAY

Check those that fall within your comfort zone:

☐ Construct a family "contact routine" through consultation with other family members. Example: Each adult child calls once each week.

☐ Keep in touch with friendly neighbors by telephone or letter. Encourage them to provide emotional support for your parent and contact with you. Send small gifts to show your appreciation. State your willingness to pay for special, consistent care when provided and appropriate.

☐ Do the same as above with friends who live in the general vicinity and can make frequent visits.

☐ Telephone on a regular basis and encourage your parent to call you regularly at your expense.

☐ Assist parent to maintain relationships from his or her end.

☐ Contact the parent's minister, priest, or rabbi and encourage them to stay in touch.

☐ Send a letter of thanks (with or without donation) to any local support group that continues to provide care services of any kind.

☐ Write upbeat letters about yourself and family on a regular basis (include pictures whenever possible).

☐ Support aging parents by remembering birthdays, anniversaries, and special holidays with cards, gifts, and telephone calls. Do the same for these individuals who provide consistent support at local level.

☐ Schedule a personal visit at least once each year. Spend as much time as possible with your parent. Also see the local support people in person. One way to do this is to have a reception for parent and invite guests.

Other suggestions:

_____

_____

_____

VULNERABILITY It is frightening how vulnerable to manipulation by family and non-family individuals frail seniors can become. Although cases of manipulation appear to be rare, seniors who reach advanced ages need some protection from a loving concerned family member.

> Mrs. Dana was victimized by her gardener and handyman for over three years before the family found out about it. When the discovery was made, almost all of Mrs. Dana's savings and some of her most priceless personal possessions were gone.

> When Clara discovered what was going on between her mother and Jennie (a grandchild from another sibling), she was shocked. Jennie, 18 years of age, was into drugs so deeply that she had drained her grandmother's finances and patience to the breaking point.

> Jake seemed so polite, sensitive, and caring about their mother that the Seaver children (three siblings) could not believe that he would disappear shortly after he and their mother were married. Along with the trauma attached to knowing she had been "duped," Mrs. Seaver had lost her sizable "nest egg" and was forced to accept help from her children.

In each of these cases it would appear that loneliness may have been part of the reason why the senior family member placed so much trust in another person. The cases are reminders to all adult children that their parents may require protection from those with dishonorable motives.

MAJOR FACTORS THAT INFLUENCE STRATEGIES Some readers, after studying and evaluating the hypothetical model, could justifiably throw up their hands and say that such a strategy wouldn't be worth the effort for their situation. These individuals could talk about how a lack of communication, geographical distance, sibling conflicts, attitudes of spouses, remarriages and/or other factors would make any strategy a waste of time in their family. But these readers may need to be reminded that even with only one aging parent and one adult child, a strategy is needed. In fact, a strategy may be more beneficial in this situation because there is more danger that the adult child could over-involve him or herself. A strategy is beneficial in *all* situations because dealing with unfinished business is normally a long-term process. Without a plan one can become totally frustrated putting out emergency fires instead of maintaining a plan that permits both parties to come out ahead with a degree of understanding and grace.

SUMMARY

1. A well-designed strategy makes it possible to provide aging parents with a superior support program, and at the same time, make it easier on siblings.

2. The "model" that was presented illustrates how a hypothetical family might develop a strategy that will help everyone prepare for the "unfinished business" that will follow. It was designed to help other families prepare a strategy to fit their unique situation.

3. Although only a few community resources were "tapped" in the model presented, it demonstrates that a community support plan should be considered as a part of any strategy.

FAMILY STUDY #17   **Reactions**

Based upon your analysis of the hypothetical strategy presented in the chapter, please answer the following questions and then match your answers with those on page 208.

How would you respond to the strategy if you were Mrs. Johnson? Mr. Johnson?

_____

_____

_____

_____

_____

_____

How would you respond if you were John, Julia, Christine, or Ray?

_____

_____

_____

_____

_____

_____

FAMILY STUDY #18   Strengths/Weaknesses

Please list what you feel the three major strengths of the strategy presented in the chapter were.

1. _____

_____

2. _____

_____

3. _____

_____

List what you feel the three biggest weaknesses were.

1. _____

_____

2. _____

_____

3. _____

_____

Compare your responses to those on page 209.

10

Loving Intervention; When And How

Adult children and friends should not anticipate intervening in the lives of loved ones as they grow older and older. It is always best when those needing help request and accept change on their own. There will be situations, however, where taking a stand may be necessary to reach the mutual goals of a support strategy. This process of intervention is not a technique unique to family situations. All of us have experienced intervention of sorts from a parent, teacher, counselor, mentor, peer or supervisor. When done in a caring, sensitive way, we usually accept it, and subsequent suggestions that are made.

We have been taught to be cautious when it comes to intervening in the lives of others. This is excellent advice, yet,

133

there are times when loving intervention is a saving grace. When a senior family member begins experiencing physical and/or mental losses, such intervention is often appreciated. Even so, the process is a delicate, (sometimes traumatic), move to take. Many factors need to be taken into consideration.

The problem is that sometimes loving intervention means that a decision is being made for an individual for the first time since childhood. We are making a judgment for another adult we dearly love. We are, in effect, taking over and assuming the consequences. So, even when we are invited to intervene, the process is touchy and, when there is some level of resistance, the process can become traumatic. Small wonder we hesitate. Even when all the signals tell us to initiate the process, our temptation is often to back away.

THE VALUE OF EARLY PRELIMINARY INTERVENTIONS

Small, beginning interventions should be viewed as welcome learning experiences that prepare adult children for the possibility of more serious interventions down the line. First you crawl, then you walk and run. And, sometimes, the value of making a small intervention during the early part of unfinished business can produce significant benefits later.

When Rod finally got up the nerve to talk to his dad about using a cane he discovered that, for the first time, communication lines opened up. Soon after they went shopping to purchase just the right cane, his father told Rod that he felt more secure about the dogs he encountered in his neighborhood walks. Later, after receiving a compliment from a lady that "the cane gave him a classy look," Rod's dad decided he wanted two canes.

Rod gained confidence by taking the first step in intervention and the Mutual Reward Theory applied — the cane was a welcome "safety factor" for his dad. The improved communications put Rod in a better position to both enjoy his dad and help him more in the future.

INTERVENTION CONSIDERATIONS As you and other members of your family contemplate the possibility of future interventions, keep the following in mind:

- Any intervention should come from the heart.

- Interventions should be a "family affair" and built into a long-term support strategy.

- The family member (or members) carrying out the intervention should be given all possible consideration and support from other family members.

- The "timing" and "method" of intervention should receive advanced planning. Intervention should never be a spur of the moment action taken by a single family member even when the "love content" is high in the relationship. A poorly devised intervention can be counter-productive.

- Where possible, interventions at all levels should be medically supported.

- It is important to recognize that many interventions involve anxiety and sadness from all parties involved. This is why it often takes the deepest love for either party to "live through" the reaction that may take place, from tears to wrath. Most interventions require a cooling off or adjustment period. Once an intervention has taken place, some relationship restoration may need to take place. In most cases relationships improve rather than deteriorate.

- Any decision made for an elderly individual who is unable to be part of the process should adhere as closely as possible to the kind of decision the party would have made in the past.

- The time to prepare for future interventions is now. The way to do this is to strengthen the relationship with communication, trust, and love when both parties can fully benefit. Sometimes intervention plans (permissions) can be put in writing.

- Some "striking out verbally" can be anticipated from the senior family member. This should be answered by stating that the intervention came from love by all family members. Consider the difference between saying "We were forced to do it" and "We were looking to your long-term comfort and happiness. Our decision was based upon our love."

- After the initial reaction has subsided, it is important to communicate how the intervention benefits the entire family. If the senior family member can see that life for others will be better (as well as their own), they may be more graceful in giving up cherished freedoms and adjust more wholesomely.

- Keep in mind that some siblings may refuse to support an intervention, yet offer no solution of their own. If you run into this situation, a family conference, attended by a family doctor or other professional, may be in order.

- Sometimes delay can be more serious than taking action.

- Who will initiate the intervention and how it will be done is sometimes more traumatic than actually doing the intervention itself.

- It is imperative that an adjustment period be anticipated and that the senior family member not, under any circumstances, feel abandoned. This means that increased communication should take place for a few days following any intervention.

- In any major intervention, assistance from a professional is recommended. If the intervention involves moving into a care facility, it is important to make a gerontologist, skilled social worker, doctor, nurse, or the manager of the facility a part of the family team.

LEVELS OF INTERVENTION The goal of all interventions, most minor, is to improve the welfare of the senior family member. Understanding that there are three levels of intervention can help one measure how much risk and preparation time may be involved, and precisely how to proceed. Listed below are specific examples of situations at the three different levels. Place a checkmark in the square opposite those situations you anticipate dealing with in the future.

Mimimum Interventions: These normally take the form of subtle hints by adult children designed to influence senior family members to either take action themselves or let others do it for them. Examples:

☐ Discontinuation of ladder or chair-climbing.

☐ Not driving a car after dark.

☐ Getting a deadbolt lock on a door.

☐ Installation of a telephone in a bedroom or bathroom.

☐ Installing rails in a bath, shower, or around a toilet.

☐ Making rugs non-skid.

☐ Putting financial and other important data where a designated family member can gain access.

☐ Preparing a will.

☐ Seeing a specialist on a medical problem.

☐ Other: _____

_____

Moderate Interventions: At this level resistance is more apt to occur, adjustment time may be longer, and the support of other family members is more important. Persuasion remains the primary technique. Examples:

☐ Convincing a senior parent to discontinue driving.

☐ Bringing in some form of community support (Meals-On-Wheels).

☐ Encouraging a move from home to an apartment, adult community, or retirement center.

☐ Getting the older person to designate power of attorney.

☐ Having someone do shopping.

☐ Accepting assistance in bill-paying.

Other: _____

_____

Major Interventions: Life-threatening situations are often present at this level. Because of this, interventions require more medical support, skill, time, sensitivity and more family involvement. Examples:

☐ Moving into adult child's home.

☐ Moving senior parent or spouse into a full-time long-term care facility — with or without consent.

☐ Taking over management of property, paying bills, and other financial matters.

☐ Assigning full-time care giver.

☐ Taking away car keys.

Other: _____

_____

As one moves from one level to another, certain dangers are present. For example, the individual being helped may develop more of a dependency relationship than is really required. Do not encourage this possibility. The longer a senior family member can function independently, the better.

As the level of interventions progress, it is important to recognize that an aging parent may voluntarily and needlessly start "giving up" freedoms she or he once cherished. This process should be discouraged at every turn. All possible independence should be maintained, or substitutes for lost freedoms should be encouraged.

INTERVENTION SIGNALS

To the caring observer, senior family members may consciously or unconsciously start sending signals that some form of assistance is welcome. These signals might include:

- When installation of safety devices around the home are requested.

- When increased concern about the future is talked about by the senior family member.

- There is a greater acceptance of assistance.

- When accusations occur, such as "you don't care what happens to me."

- If different family members are given bits of information that sound like a call for help.

- When there are changes in eating and/or sleeping habits.

- If different socialization habits begin to take place.

- When problems result from failure to take action, such as leaving bills unpaid.

- Whenever there may be a sudden refusal to see a doctor, or secrecy about visiting a doctor.

- When there is forgetfulness about things usually remembered.

- Whenever on-going changes in grooming habits appear.

- If there are increases in arguments, or situations that alienate others.

- When a multiplication of ills and ailments takes place.

- Whenever unexplained bruises appear that could indicate a fall.

Other: _____

_____

_____

INTERPRETATION OF SIGNALS AND "WATCH AREAS"

Properly interpreted, the signals that aging parents send out can tell us when they might resist or accept intervention and just when a family conference might be in order. Some signals may be deliberately transmitted. Others may be subconscious.

An adult child can "pick up" on the signals by being aware of certain "watch areas." Grooming is an example. Standards of grooming can slowly deteriorate on an accelerated basis as the elderly parent moves through the three levels of intervention. Other "watch areas" are presented in the following exercise.

INTERVENTION EXERCISE

Study the situation in the following paragraph and answer the questions in the spaces provided.

> Of the four siblings in your family, you have developed the best relationship with your mother. Slowly, over the past five years, your mother (now in her eighties) has become increasingly frail. The signals of concern are appearing in five watch areas. These have been communicated to other family members.
>
> Your mother has lived in her own home for the past forty years, and seems aware that the time is near when she must either accept some outside help or leave her home. She refuses to talk about it, however.
>
> One of her medical problems is poor vision. Yesterday, the family doctor recommended a cataract operation. Your mother refuses to consider it, saying, "I am too old and won't be around long anyway. Just leave me alone."

Is there an ethical issue here that should be taken up with other family members? Does the mother have a right to deny the operation?

_____

_____

_____

What issues need to be brought to the attention of the entire family?

_____

_____

_____

What intervention approach will gain the greatest degree of cooperation from your mother?

_____

_____

_____

Who should do the intervention? How should it be done?

_____

_____

_____

What kind of post-operative support system needs to be developed?

_____

_____

_____

PROGRESSIVE INTERVENTION GUIDE

This exercise is designed to help family members trace signals in certain "watch areas" through the three levels of intervention. Naturally, the more signals received in the various watch areas the faster the elderly parent is moving into intervention level 2 or 3. A few specific suggestions are made at level 1 and 2; but when an individual reaches level 3 in more than one area, the options decrease. The reader is reminded that each situation has its own elements and that this exercise is simply a guide. Even when signals have intensified in many watch areas, professional outsiders should be consulted.

WATCH AREA	LEVEL 1	LEVEL 2	LEVEL 3
Pill planning becoming confused	Get a pill planner	Move in caretaker	
Diet disintegration. Unable to prepare proper meals	Help in cooking	Meals-on-Wheels	
Disorientation	Provide visual clues		*Move Into*
Increased falling	More hand-rails, walker		*Your Own*
			Home,
Increase in financial mistakes	Assist	Do it yourself	*Retirement*
Grooming	Discuss	Help	*Center*
Increased isolation; does not enjoy or watch television anymore	Discuss	See professionals	*or Other*
Marked increase in physical disorders	Check with doctor		*Care*
DIFFERENT SIGNALS YOU NOTICE AND YOUR RECOMMENDED ACTIONS			*Facility*
_____			
_____			

TECHNIQUES OF INTERVENTION
Assume you have a delicate matter to discuss with an aging parent, such as something dealing with the health, safety, or well-being of that individual which requires some intervention on your part. You intend to be as non-directive and sensitive as possible; but taking the first step is almost more than you can handle. You have been worried about how to approach the subject for days.

Please read all of the techniques presented below and select the three that best fit your "comfort zone." Do this by placing a check in the appropriate square.

☐ **Ask a Favor:** "Mom, would you do me a favor and have your hearing checked?"

☐ **Worried/Worried Technique:** "Mother, I've been so worried about your having an accident driving on the freeway that I have been unable to sleep at night. Can we talk about it?"

☐ **Planting an Idea:** "Dad, how is your friend, Harry, getting along in the new retirement center?"

☐ **Asking a Question:** "Have you given any thought to selling your home so you can take advantage of your once-in-a-lifetime tax exclusion?"

☐ **Assuming a Decision Has Been Made:** "We will both enjoy our conversations more when you have a hearing aid."

☐ **Offer to Pay:** "I'll be happy to pick up the tab for the best hearing instrument available."

☐ **Permission to Consult Others:** "Regarding the problem we discussed yesterday, do I have your permission to talk it over with the rest of the family?"

☐ **Setting the Stage:** "We need to get together with your lawyer over this situation. If you wish, I will call and make the appointment."

☐ **Serious Talk Ahead:** "We keep delaying your plans for the future. The next time we meet we must have a serious talk. In the meantime, let's think through the options on our own so we will be prepared."

IF NONE OF THE TECHNIQUES APPEAL TO YOU OR FIT YOUR SITUATION, USE YOUR FAVORITES AS MODELS AND DEVISE YOUR OWN.

SUMMARY

1. Any form of intervention should be based on love. The real needs of aging parents must be considered. Facts to back up any intervention are essential (such as medical evaluations). Signals that have been observed and discussed by key family members are often a beginning clue that intervention is needed. Consideration of aging parents and the family as a whole is important.

2. There are three levels of intervention that are often, (but not always), progressive in nature. They are (1) minimum, (2) moderate, and (3) major.

3. There are various techniques of intervention that can help family members get the process started. Nothing should be done, however, until a family dialogue takes place regarding what is needed and how the solution will be implemented and communicated.

FAMILY STUDY #19 **Raymond Brings His Mother Home**

An only child, Raymond has always felt a special love and responsibility for his mother. When he lost his father, Raymond made many trips back to Fayetteville, Arkansas from his home in San Francisco. He never fails to telephone his mom one or two times each week.

Fortunately, Raymond's mother has been a strong person who has stayed involved with many friends. Living in the family home alone has not been a problem until last month when she broke her hip falling on a slippery floor. Sensing this might be the beginning of further deterioration, Raymond, with the consent and cooperation of his wife and their three college-age children, decided to bring his mother into their large home.

During his vacation, Raymond returned to Arkansas and placed the family home for sale. He also arranged to sell most of his mother's possessions before bringing her back with him to San Francisco.

Although everyone did their best to make Grandma feel wanted, needed, and at home, she became less active than anyone anticipated, and within a few months was spending most of her time alone in her room. Less than a year later, it was decided to place her in a skilled nursing center where she could receive the best possible attention.

In looking back, Raymond told his wife; "Well, bringing Grandma out here was the right thing to do because she wouldn't have made it very long back there alone."

Do you agree? Write out your answer and match it with the interpretation on page 209.

_____

_____

_____

_____

_____

FAMILY STUDY #20   Solution For Ralph

Ralph is an easy-going individual who has been content to leave most decisions to his wife, Martha. Both in their late sixties, they invited Martha's mother, Helen, to come and live with them last November. Helen is 91, and until very recently, was doing extremely well. During the past month, there has been a general deterioration in Helen's health. The family doctor has not been specific as to a problem; and Helen's needs have increased daily.

At this point, Ralph is more worried about Martha's health than that of his mother-in-law. Martha has assumed the duties of a nurse and it is beginning to have an effect. On top of everything else, Helen has become increasingly demanding, which frustrates Martha.

For the past couple of weeks, Ralph has been quietly investigating various local health care facilities. The best choice seems to be a nursing home within walking distance of their home.

Twice last week Ralph suggested to Martha that Helen move to the home for her own good as well as theirs. Each time he made this suggestion, Martha has broken into tears and left the room. Nothing has been accomplished.

Ralph was unable to sleep last night trying to figure out whether or not he should put his foot down and intervene. He finally decided on four options: (1) talk to Martha about his needs; (2) talk openly and frankly with both Martha and her mother about the absolute necessity of a move; (3) call a family meeting (Martha has two sisters and a brother), present all the facts, and seek support for the move; (4) without telling his wife, consult with the family doctor and have him counsel Martha on taking care of her own health first, and that of her mother second.

Do you agree that it is time for Ralph to force a decision? Which of the options do you like best? How would you prioritize them? Write out how you would deal with the situation and then compare your answer with the interpretation on page 211.

11

Care Options; Investigate With An Open Mind

"I'm in the prime of senility."
Joel Chandler Harris

Years ago, it was common practice for adult children to invite "grandma and/or grandpa" to live with them. This practice has continued and is likely to increase if housing and health care costs continue to escalate. For some nuclear families it is an ideal solution, permitting a more frequent expression of love by all parties, more personal care for the aging parents, and in some cases, less strain on financial budgets. The conditions for success, however, should meet certain standards as pointed out in the following exercise.

Inviting Parents to Live With You — The decision to share your home with a parent is a major one and should be made only after considerable communication, especially with the

147

older person, has taken place, and there are positive indicators that things will "work."

Listed below are three primary considerations. If a sincere "yes" answer can be provided to all three questions, the possibilities appear promising. A single "no" indicates caution.

1. **Will the mutual reward theory apply between the aging parent and all family members?** Having a parent in a home only works when rewards are given and accepted by all parties. The aging parent must contribute and feel needed and the rest of the family must be willing to provide rewards in return (especially being a good listener and having "fun together"). If you are certain MRT will operate, place a check in the "yes" box.

    YES ☐   NO ☐

2. **Will the aging parent become a full member of the family?** Some adult children invite their parents to join them and then proceed to put them in a corner where they become isolated and dejected. Unless the parent can communicate openly and frequently with all family members, the situation will soon become uncomfortable. If all family members are willing to provide full membership, place a check in the appropriate box.

    YES ☐   NO ☐

3. **Is the "host" family sufficiently solid to make it work?** This is a difficult question to ask and answer. If a marriage is shaky to begin with, the chances of successfully adding a senior member are less likely. Second marriages and/or when children from a previous family are present, are high risk environments. And when the financial advantages are permitted to weigh heavily on a decision, the risk of failure accelerates.

    YES ☐   NO ☐

As difficult as the decision may be to invite a parent to live with you, a more difficult and traumatic decision is to move an aging parent into a health care facility. Although residents can and do move in and out of nursing homes and retirement centers, the possibility that this might be the last move is hard to hide. The finality is felt on both sides of the relationship and the matter is extremely sensitive to discuss.

Sometimes (unfortunately), the move is made in an unplanned manner, usually out of a sense of obligation or guilt. When this happens, resentments are prone to surface and relationships often deteriorate. *Any move into a health care facility is a major intervention and should be undertaken with planning, utilization of multiple resources, and advanced communication and counseling.*

WHAT IS AVAILABLE? The first step is to openly discuss the advantages and disadvantages of a move based on the care facilities that are available in (or near) the community where the aging parent now resides. To help prepare you for such a search, place a check opposite the possibility you and senior involved feel offers the greatest promise.

☐ **Retirement Living Centers.** These sometimes luxurious (and expensive) facilities are geared for the more active senior family member, stressing independence within apartment-like living spaces, often with maid service. Most have activity programs and social services. Some will provide one complete meal and some nursing care. Wide variety of other services.*

☐ **Life Care Facilities.** Certain retirement centers combine into one location several living options, including life care facilities. In other words, the resident can move into other units in a progressive manner, if and when greater care is required. Such facilities present a once-in-a-lifetime choice at an earlier stage. Careful investigation is recommended. Some require a "buy in" provision that only a few can afford.

---

* In making a final decision on any care facility, the *Care Facility Appraisal Exercise* on page 155 can be most helpful.

☐ **Residential Care.** These are often referred to as Board and Care facilities and are usually found in residential homes under government supervision. Most provide nurse-aid services such as bathing and dressing assistance. Continency is expected. Some lightly confused but active persons are accepted in these settings when "wandering" is not a problem. Although "loving care" in a home climate is the goal, prior investigation is suggested.

☐ **Intermediate Care.** The main difference here is that around-the-clock care is provided. Some skilled nursing homes have a portion of their facility devoted to intermediate care. This type of facility is required to be licensed. Guests are expected to be mobile and able to to do some things.

☐ **Skilled Nursing or Extended Care.** These facilities are most commonly known as nursing homes. They provide 24-hour nursing services. This can be the most expensive alternative. This kind of care is useful after hospitalization, when home care is too extensive or when the health of the person is apt to be jeopardized. They often turn out to be long-term care facilities.

☐ **Locked Facilities.** These are licensed and equipped to take care of patients who have mental and emotional problems, and who are extremely confused and tend to wander. Locked means that exits and entrances are locked and keys or alarms are used to protect patients.

How can you find what is available in your locality? A good place to begin is to consult your doctor, social workers, Department of Health, senior centers, library, or church or temple. Also, look under retirement, hospitals, rest homes and nursing homes in your Yellow Pages.

It should be pointed out that respite care can be furnished by most of the alternatives listed above. Respite care is designed to give both adult children and senior family members a "break" or "breathing sell." This kind of care can also delay the making of more permanent decisions. An added advantage is that such temporary "care" can break down some of the negativity connected with commitment to a long-term facility.

AN UNUSUAL OPTION

In Los Angeles there is a non-profit organization called Alternative Living for the Aging. This group leases a large home where eight seniors (five women and three men) live in a group household arrangement. Residents pay $395.00 monthly for a private room and bath, five dinners a week, and partial house-cleaning service.*

If such an arrangement were available in your community would you, as an older senior, be interested? As an adult child, can you see an aging parent in this environment?

A number of advantages are possible, including: (1) retaining a degree of independence, (2) socialization opportunities, (3) availability of immediate support when needed, (4) low cost, and (5) some responsibility for residents and some supervision. The major disadvantage could be the selection of the right "mix" of residents.

Compared to other types of "senior living environments," a group household may be preferred over a "nursing residence," which is regulated and requires the availability of a trained nurse at all times. Are group households a viable alternative? Test your feelings with the statements below.

As an aging senior, I can/cannot see myself living in a group household environment.

As an adult child, I can/cannot see my parent(s) living in a group household environment.

If such an opportunity were available, I would/would not like to investigate the possibility.

* Rents are higher in Los Angeles than most U.S. communities.

PROTECTING THE DIGNITY OF THE AGING INDIVIDUAL

As humans, we have certain rights. When we honor these rights with others, we dignify ourselves. It is only natural that we be a little more protective about the rights of members in our own family circles. This is especially true when people may not be able to fight for their own rights.

When we search for the best possible care facility for a senior family member, it is important to be aware of the rights we and our loved ones expect. Residents of care facilities have special rights protected by the Department of Health (normally a state responsibility). You can help facilitate this "trust agreement" by knowing in advance just what rights your loved one is entitled to receive.

It is equally important to ascertain the rights of the facility and their expectations from you as a participant.

Each family member admitted to a nursing home has a right to:*

- be treated with dignity and respect, including privacy in treatment and in conducting personal affairs.

- associate and communicate freely with persons of their choice, including clergy, lawyers, and family members — unless a physician deems it is harmful to health.

- be free of mental and physical abuse, and from chemical and physical restraints (except for emergencies) authorized in writing by the physician.

- be fully informed of the facility's fees and practices.

- be fully informed of services available and all charges.

- be fully informed of their medical condition by a physician, and have the opportunity to participate in planning of medical treatment. They should also be aware of the right to refuse treatment and understand the consequences of such refusal. Finally, there is the right to refuse to participate in experimental research.

- retain use of personal clothing and possessions as space permits, unless to do so would infringe on the rights of others.

---

* Adapted from Skilled Nursing Facilities Regulations, California Administrative Code Title 22, Division 5, Chapter 2.

- have reasonable access to telephone communication.

- privacy for visits and the opportunity to share the same room with spouses when desired.

To determine the nursing home resident's rights for your State, contact the State Department of Health. Most facilities have such rights posted in plain sight.

WHEN ABUSE IS FOUND Should you notice any form of mistreatment to your family member (or other resident), go immediately to the administrator of that facility so corrective action will be initiated. When you make such a report, keep these three factors in mind: (1) abuse — whether it be physical, emotional or financial — is often difficult to "pin down;" (2) you may need to draw support interpreting state laws; and using any available "hot lines", or legal and other guidance services; (3) facilities often have written guidance procedures.

HEALTH CARE FACILITY APPRAISAL EXERCISE Selecting a care facility is similar to choosing a college for a daughter. Consider these questions:

Which (facility or college) has the highest standards?
Which (manor or dormitory) has the best physical layout?
Which has the best recreational facilities?
Does the institution promote individual well-being?
Which environment fits the resident best?

Other comparisons are possible, *including cost.* And just as every student should be totally involved in the choice of her or his college, the future resident of a care facility should be involved in the selection process.

This exercise is designed to help you select the best care facility for a parent, friend, or, since you are likely to be lucky enough to live that long, *yourself.*

The exercise assumes that the costs of facilities are equal. (They may not be. Facilities have different daily and monthly rates. Payment can be totally private or covered to varying degrees by state programs. What help Medicare A & B provide will need to be investigated. All financial aspects should be explored and careful comparisons made independent of the exercise that follows.)

Preliminary Tips

Tip #1: Give each facility the opportunity to put its best foot forward. To help this happen, call in the morning for an afternoon appointment (mornings are often for baths, therapy, general housekeeping, etc.). Try to arrive with a positive attitude. If you (or your loved one) feel tired, out-of-sorts, or negative, wait until another day.

Tip #2: Make a special effort to approach each visit relaxed and casual. Make the point of asking the same questions (those in the exercise). Do not take the exercise into the facility, but complete it soon after your visit. Both you and your loved one should do it together.

Tip #3. A good rule is to observe without prying. Notice especially how residents are treated by staff. Be friendly to everyone, and feel free to speak to residents. If they are responsive, you are getting a positive sign.

Tip #4: Do not expect your loved one to be highly positive about a visitation. This is a very difficult decision for anyone, even under ideal circumstances. Adjustment time is required. Of course, if she or he says "this is where I want to be", no further visitations may be necessary.

Instructions

Rate each of the ten factors on a scale from 10 to 1 for each facility. A 10 rating indicates perfect; a 5 rating is average; a 3 or below is a strong negative reaction. All factors are weighted equally.

FACTOR	FACILITY #1	FACILITY #2	FACILITY #3
Compassion: Some facilities train their staff to express their natural concern for residents. This extra love is demonstrated by touching and the tone of voice. The more of this you sense, the higher the rating you should award.			
Environment: Facilities have the capacity to create a warm, happy atmosphere. If you hear laughter, music, singing, or sense that there is a lively staff that enjoys being with residents, you can give this factor a high rating.			
Medical: Although State standards are rigid, you will want to verify the reputation of each facility through five sources. (1) Ask the administrator to discuss their professional standards. (2) Ask your own doctor and at least one other. (3) Ask to see the latest state survey (which should be posted). (4) Check with local ombudsman. (5) Observe how well cared for the residents appear.			
Physical: Room size, openness, nearness to bed-mates, brightly painted rooms, sunlight/electrical lighting, access to bathroom, size and decor of recreation and dining rooms, outside patios and gardens — even parking for visitors is a factor to be considered. Can resident have his or her own television? Chair? Wall pictures? The tour you receive will give you the signals you need to make this rating.			
Cleanliness: Clues are clean bed linens, floors, bathrooms, and above all, the cleanliness for residents. An older facility may be cleaner than a newer one because management has higher standards.			

FACTOR	FACILITY #1	FACILITY #2	FACILITY #3
Recreation: Some facilities do a much better job in providing meaningful, adaptable, and enjoyable recreational opportunities for residents. Through education, exercise, religious, and entertainment programs, residents can remain active. Rate this factor carefully.			
Meals: For some residents, meals are the highlight of the day. What is a typical menu? How much variety? How served? What about dietary standards? Extend your visit or return later so you can observe a meal period. Do those who need help in eating receive it?			
Geographical: The nearer a resident can be to his or her inner circle of relatives and friends, the better; it makes it easier for friends to visit and visitations are significant events. You may wish to give the facility with the best location a 10 and then rate the others lower. Also, how close the facility is to public transportation should be considered.			
Freedom: Although you want your loved one to be fully protected from injury, the more freedom to move around the better. For example, is there an outside garden accessible? What about the problem of roommate compatibility? Ask if there are changes made to deal with incompatibility. Are there any restrictions on visiting hours? The more flexibility you sense, the higher the rating for this factor.			
Comfort zone: People of all ages feel better and more secure in their own "comfort zones." If one facility has a "homey atmosphere" where another tries to be more of a country club, the future resident should rate the one highest that best fits his or her individual comfort zone.			
TOTAL SCORES			

A rating of 80 or above is exceptionally high. A rating under 50 may indicate a second visit is in order. Please keep in mind that this exercise is designed only as a guide to make an extremely difficult decision.

In addition to the rating procedure, you should check on the reputation of the facility in the community, seek opinions by hospital discharge planners and ombudsmen, and check any local "survey reports" that may be on file. Talk with other families who have members as guests — solicit their feedback.

TIPS ON VISITING A LOVED ONE

When it comes to sustaining and enhancing a relationship with a senior family member, nothing means more than a personal visit. To a confined person, a friendly visit is a breath of fresh air — a signal that others still care and that life can continue to have meaning.

Of course, making a visit successful often takes some preparation on the part of the visitor. For example, if you are a good listener, are positive, and try to meet the needs of the loved one, the visit will probably go well. If, however, you anticipate trouble or dread the visit in the first place, the visit could be upsetting to both parties.

There are only two times when it might be best not to make a visit: (1) when you really do not want to go; or (2) when you are going out of guilt. Nobody wants to receive visitors who come against their will; this attitude is usually transmitted during the visit and the experience will probably be counter-productive.

Although an attempt should be made to make each visit a good experience — one in which both parties laugh and enjoy themselves — remember that senior family members often have deeper needs than does the visitor. Sharing these concerns — including family problems, increased illness, or unfinished business — are vital. When one is troubled inside, there is a demanding need to talk to someone you love and trust. This is especially true when the visitor is a spouse.

Listed below are some tips on how you might make future visits mutually rewarding. Place a check opposite any ideas you would feel comfortable using.

☐ Make the visit out of love and concern.

☐ Visit with an attitude of *high expectancy*. The more you anticipate a successful visit, the more apt it is to happen.

☐ Arrive prepared to relate something interesting that the resident will identify with easily.

☐ Listen with both your eyes and your heart. Do less than 50% of the talking yourself.

☐ Find out quickly if something is troubling the resident so they can get it off their chests early in the meeting. If it is therapeutic for the senior family member, be prepared to listen patiently to some sadness and grief. Sometimes a resident is desperate to have a serious conversation and to be taken seriously in return. If complaints drag on, you might set a "cut-off" point.

☐ When a problem surfaces that requires action, play the role of a sensitive counselor. Do your best to help the loved one come up with his or her own solution. If they are unable to convert a decision into action, do it for them.

☐ When a negative or painful conversation has reached the point where you know it will not be productive to continue, change the subject to something more positive. Do not let a communications session drag on in a negative way.

☐ Communicate your care through holding hands, a kiss, or a pat. Touching is a verification to the elderly person that they are important and still retain their identify.

☐ Look for something personal that is deserving of a comment or compliment. *Notice the individual.*

☐ Take time to be pleasant and upbeat to staff members without becoming a bother. Compliment good work or special attention. The more they like you, the more apt they are to do extra things for your loved one — *after you have gone.*

☐ Report any lack of proper care directly to the manager. DO THIS IN A FRIENDLY COOPERATIVE MANNER and be as clear as possible about what you want changed. See residents' rights on page 152. Follow up at a later date.

☐ Revere and appreciate the past experiences of the elderly person. View what they communicate as a private history lesson. Reminiscing can be fun and comforting. Some repetition is to be expected and can often be enjoyed by both parties a second time around.

☐ Consider each visit as a research opportunity to learn more about the aging process. This attitude can help you age more gracefully yourself.

☐ Visit often, but not so often that the resident becomes over-dependent on you and your visits (or you start to become negative yourself). Although any visit is a good visit, guard against a long series of "quickies" that seem to relieve your guilt feelings but makes the resident feel your visits are based on obligation instead of love. A quick visit is less likely to be mutually rewarding than a longer one where there has been real communication.

☐ Leave at a high point; never drag a visit out too long. Thirty to 45 minutes is quality time — beyond that things can go downhill.

☐ Occasionally, bring someone else with you that the resident knows personally or knows about because of you. It is often refreshing for a shut-in to meet a new personality.

☐ Give your visits variety — walk together, sit in the garden, peruse magazines, pray together, attend activities together. Give the resident the pleasure of introducing you to others.

☐ When possible, go on outings together —shopping, eating out, visiting an old friend.

The goal is to make each visit a special event for both the resident and yourself. Of course, you cannot expect a visit to be special every time. Normally, you should feel better after a visit. You should be able to take the rewards you received with you and enhance your own lifestyle. If this rarely happens, it might be a good idea to review the suggestions above. You may discover you have fallen into some bad habits that can be reversed on your next visit. Keep in mind that the above tips are equally appropriate to aging parents living in their own homes or less formal residential care arrangements.

INFREQUENT BUT CONCENTRATED VISITS MAY BE A BETTER ANSWER

Some adult children, primarily those who live nearby, mistakenly believe that frequent "quickie" visitations with elderly parents are the most rewarding type of visit. This may be the case when caregiving is involved; however, in other situations it may be just the opposite.

Jim, because he lives on the East Coast, sees his mother in San Diego only twice a year. But, on each visit he gives his mother three days of undivided attention. He takes her out to lunch, and they have every opportunity to discuss serious problems. When Jim leaves for the airport, both he and his mother feel happy and fulfilled.

Joyce lives close to her mother, but as a busy executive who travels a lot, the visits are usually two or three weeks apart. When Joyce does make a visit, she calls ahead and devotes a full afternoon, doing anything her mother wishes. Joyce sees that there is plenty of time for a serious conversation. Both she and her mother find the arrangement more rewarding than frequent, short meetings.

Caroline and Jack live two thousand miles away from his father. Their solution is spending a full week each spring at the home doing every possible odd job that has accumulated.

Clarence takes his mother on a vacation each year. This is often the only time he sees her. Would she trade for more frequent shorter visits? Not on your life!

Mary Lou could see her father once or twice a week if necessary, but her father prefers that they attend Mass once a month and have a good talk afterward.

Although each situation is different, infrequent visits where the adult child gives his or her parent full attention may accomplish a better feeling than short, in and out, visits. The meaningfulness of the contact and not the frequency needs to be considered.

SUMMARY

1. A wide variety of care facilities can be found in most communities — everything from board and care to lifetime full-care retirement centers. A facility that fits both the financial and environmental comfort zone of the prospective resident will be most beneficial to all concerned.

2. Care should be taken to make a complete and thorough investigation of local care facilities before a decision is made. Both the elderly parent and other family members should be involved. Completing the health care facility appraisal exercise is recommended.

3. Once located, regular visitations from friends and family are vital for the best possible adjustment. There are many techniques that can help make a visit mutually rewarding.

RELIEVE THE PRESSURE BY USING SUBSTITUTES

As an adult child, it is easy to lock yourself into a rigid visitation schedule to aging parents. This is especially true if the parent is institutionalized, and within easy driving distance. The good part is that the parent can look forward to seeing you on a predictable schedule. The bad part is that you may stifle your own life and lifestyle.

Solution?

Consider working in a substitute visitor so that, when you are on vacation, a business trip, ill, or just too busy to relax enough to enjoy a visit, your "substitute" can take over. One way to do this is to take a friend with you for a few visits, and if the friend and your parent like each other, you have a prospective substitute. Of course, arrangements need to be made. If your friend volunteers, then there should be some kind of recognition or reward for their contribution. If it becomes necessary to ask someone to play the role of a substitute, then an appropriate financial arrangement may be in order. The kind of reward depends upon the situation.

Friends, family members, neighbors who are also seniors, retirees who may frequent senior centers and could use some extra money, and church members, can all make suitable substitutes.

Everyone can benefit from a substitute arrangement! You get the freedom you need, your parent gets to communicate with more than one person, and the substitute will learn about the aging process. If all goes well, you and the substitute can have a separate rewarding relationship based on your visitation and sometimes care-giving experiences.

FAMILY STUDY #21   **Mrs. Ames's Friend Hugo**

Mrs. Ames is steadfast in refusing to enter a local nursing home because she can't take her friend of twelve years with her, a loving but aging collie named Hugo.

The nursing home will not admit Hugo because he is a large dog and his age and long hair would require special care.

To eliminate the obstacle the family has volunteered to care for Hugo in the best possible manner.

Although the family realizes that the increasing disabled condition of Mrs. Ames will eventually bring her to the decision to leave Hugo in good hands, everyone is extremely nervous about the situation. The signals, supported by the family doctor, indicate the move is already overdue. And, although no one has the nerve to mention it, it has been obvious for some time that Mrs. Ames is not up to taking good care of Hugo any longer.

What suggestions would you make to the Ames family to solve their problem with Hugo? Is there a reward exchange involved? Please write out your ideas below and then study those on page 211.

FAMILY STUDY #22   Katherine's Attitude

Katherine's husband is a highly successful executive. Their two children and three grandchildren are supportive family members. When Katherine is not playing golf and entertaining at the local country club, she is often with her mother, Helen, now residing in the most expensive nursing home in town. A devoted daughter, Katherine naturally wants her mother to have the finest of care. But, of all the adult children with parents in the home, Katherine is the least popular among the manager and staff. The reason is based on comments like these:

"I want you to keep my mother away from those old sick people."

"My mother is to receive her meals in the privacy of her own room."

"I just don't want my mother mixing with others in those silly recreational activities."

How might Katherine's attitude be harming instead of helping her mother? Write out your reasons and compare them with those on page 212.

_____

_____

_____

_____

_____

_____

_____

12

Sharing The
Ultimate Victory

*"Colors fade, temples crumble, empires fall, but wise
words endure."*
Edward Thorndike

Most people enjoy victories, and most receive several during
their lives — school graduation, athletic trophies, creative
citations, personal acclaims, career successes, and/or recognition at retirement. The ultimate victory may come later in
life, and it may make previous victories seem insignificant.

The victory I have in mind is becoming a Master Senior.
This is an honor earned *after* a person has made a success of
retirement, not before. It is a special achievement reserved for
a select few.

Academia bestows advanced degrees on those who achieve
high standards in science, the arts, business or other
disciplines. Why not use a similar designation to identify
those who struggle and find meaning in their late years?

Why not award honorary degrees to seniors who survive with dignity? Why not find a way to recognize a person who fits the following description?

> **Master Senior:** A person who earns respect through late-in-life involvements. Someone who experiences personal growth following retirement. One who accepts the challenge of aging and stays physically active and mentally positive. A person who becomes a senior role model.

Retirement is a signal for many to drift through later years without continuing the use of their talents. Some individuals refuse to set any meaningful goals or accept even modest challenges. These individuals become part of the "lost" senior generation. Those who continue to make the most of their lives earn the right to be called Master Seniors. They refuse to rest on their early-life laurels.

Like earning a Master's Degree from a prestigious university, becoming a Master Senior is demanding. It is not easy to discard previous forms of recognition and start over to achieve new ones. How many of us can create a new image that will earn respect when we are in a new environment with new rules — especially when all of this must be accomplished while the aging process is accelerating?

Mrs. Drake (now 86) earned the right to be called a Master Senior through community and church involvement while, during the same period, she was fighting off recurring cancer.

Mr. Vargus (now 82) earned his "degree" through 15 years of leadership as a volunteer activity director in a modest mobile home park. He has spent the past two years as director from a wheelchair.

> Mr. and Mrs. Rice (both 85) earned their citations by conducting a support group for singles age 60 and over. This was accomplished during a 20-year period when efforts to curtail the "aging process" was a daily battle.
>
> Mrs. Smith (now 92) earned her recognition by holding her large family together against great odds. This was accomplished through patience, understanding, and compassion.

Master Seniors can earn their title in countless ways. Some will do it through creative efforts in photography, painting, or writing. Others through loyal service within organizations or on a personal basis. A few desire recognition for simply being strong and "giving" of themselves. Others by surviving without bitterness. Some by being caring grandparents. There is no prescribed curriculum.

Master Seniors are often quiet, unassuming people (non-celebrities). Most are at least 80 years of age and have won battles on both the physical and psychological sides of aging. Of course, many who achieve Master Senior status owe much of their good fortune to sound health. Others would also have achieved the ultimate victory if terminal illness did not remove them from the competition, but this should take nothing away from those who did survive. The individual victories of the survivors should not be denied.

Where can you find a Master Senior?

Actually, they are very easy to meet. Many remain in their own homes, often caring for an ailing spouse. Others live gracefully with an adult child. Still others live active lives in retirement centers or nursing homes.

How can Master Seniors be identified? Here are some personal characteristics they often have in common. In reading them, you may wish to make a commitment to work toward earning your Master Senior degree one day.

Despite pain and adversity, Master Seniors stay in charge of their own lives for as long as it is safe and smart to do so.

Regardless of income, they live with dignity and style.

They pursue goals and activities with a positive outlook and enthusiasm.

Master Seniors do all they can to maintain good health through exercise and diet. During periods of illness, they fight back so that they will not lose excessive ground to the aging process.

They continue to learn. Many attend Elder Hostel seminars, and community workshops. They contribute to the lives of others (especially those younger) so that, as needed, they have constructed a multi-generational support system.

Master Seniors can often be identified by their sense of humor. They seldom complain and are fun to be near.

TOUGH COOKIE

The term "tough cookie" has been around for a long time. There are many applications for the phrase. Only recently, however, have seniors used it to depict themselves. Now it is possible to see the twinkle in the eyes of even a frail senior as he or she says with pride, "I didn't get this far without being a tough cookie." It is encouraging to hear.

In some cases, the expression is simply a bold statement of independence to outsiders to hide some fears or misgivings inside. It is a self-defense mechanism that declares, "Look, I've learned to cope over the years, and you would be wise to take this into consideration."

What the expression really says is that the individual is willing to accept support if presented in the right way. Being a "tough cookie" doesn't mean "stay away from me," it means "respect me for where I have been and what I represent." Tough cookies can survive without your love and support, but it would be wonderful to have it.

When enough age has been added, tough cookies turn into delightfully beautiful people. And some can still turn out "home made cookies" that you can't equal at the local bakery.

It is not uncommon to hear individuals, (especially those in the entertainment industry) talk about being "survivors." This usually means they have taken their bumps in a tough profession and are still performing. Good for them! But surviving for an extended lifetime and then performing well is a challenge of a different dimension. True Master Seniors do this! And ideally each could receive national recognition. Of course, it is not possible to arrange mass graduations or present Master Senior degrees to those who have qualified. There are, however, some practical alternatives.

- Communities and retirements centers could establish Master Senior days and make presentations to new members who have qualified.

- Families could start paying the ultimate compliment: "Grandma, you are a true Master Senior." "Gramps, you are a great role model for me, and in my book, a Master Senior."

- If formal recognition is not forthcoming, those who feel they qualify could start including an M.S. after their names on stationery and personal cards.

Many Master Seniors might not feel comfortable with forms of recognition such as those suggested above. Sometimes, having a "grace period" of understanding and appreciation by others might be all the reward they desire. The word "grace" implies a kind of spirituality that is granted to a few toward the end of their lives. This should be a period of special beauty, superior insight, acceptance — a spiritual "act of payment." Grace, in this sense, permits one to feel at ease with her or his mortality. For many, this inner peace and tranquility, recognized or not, will be the ultimate victory.

Master Seniors are willing, when encouraged, to share their victories and failures with children, grandchildren, friends, and/or professional caretakers. Most can be encouraged to communicate their insights and wisdom in order to enhance the growth of others. In the right situation, Master Seniors may share feelings. Such as what it is like to "grow old" so that others can benefit. Some can give suggestions on how others might benefit from searching for their own style of "late in life" victory. Master Seniors have much to offer and usually are willing to share, providing they are invited to do so.

SUMMARY

1. A Master Senior is an individual who experiences measurable personal growth after retirement. Most are age eighty or older. Master Seniors are easy to find, especially when you have one in your own family.

2. Master Seniors deserve more recognition from all sources.

3. One can learn a great deal about life and the aging process from a Master Senior.

FAMILY STUDY #23   Silent Victory

With only occasional visits and limited communication from family members, Mrs. Denver lived her final years gracefully in a nursing home. Toward the end, she lost interest in television and group activities and spent most of her time reminiscing and musing to herself.

Mrs. Denver looked forward to therapy days, not so much because of the physical part, but because she had someone to talk with. On occasion her minister would come by and they could talk. But Mrs. Denver felt her days were enriched primarily because of Maisie, a practical nurse assigned to her wing. Maisie was an ideal caregiver. Everything she did had love attached to it. Most of all Maisie would listen. This was especially true when Maisie, on her non-working days, would take Mrs. Denver for drives in the country and "let her ramble."

It was therefore no surprise to close observers when Mrs. Denver left a sizable part of her estate to Maisie. After the funeral, two of Mrs. Denver's children discussed the matter. Joel, the oldest son, said: "I"m pleased mother took good care of Maisie . She was there the last few years with love and understanding when mother needed her. Maisie went far beyond her professional obligation."

Genevieve, the youngest daughter, replied: "I'm not so sure. All of us kids missed out on discussions that could have been rewarding if we had been able to squeeze out the time. I see no reason why we should share our inheritance, especially with a professional."

Do you agree with Joel or Genevieve? State your position below and compare your answer with that of the author on page 212.

_____

_____

_____

_____

_____

_____

_____

_____

_____

FAMILY STUDY #24   Regrets

Last week, Genelle, Marty, and Sam were discussing their mother who died three years ago. Genelle, the senior sibling, who was age 70, said: "The thing I regret is that I didn't make more time to spend with mother, especially during the final months. I feel now that there was much she wanted to share about her spirituality, and death."

Marty replied: "I agree. Mother had a lot of answers to aging that gerontologists seem to know little about. The sad part is that we never gave her a chance to tell us."

Sam however said: "You are both suffering from needless remorse. You can't prepare for old age by listening to old people, even if that person happens to be your mother. The way to get ready for the final years, is to live the early phases of life to the fullest. Our mother knew this. She would have had too much class to tell us that being old is a disaster."

Do you agree with Genelle and Marty? Or with Sam? Should people plan for the final years like they do for retirement? Do older people have aging secrets to share? State your views below and then compare them with those on page 213.

_____

_____

_____

_____

_____

_____

_____

13

Finishing Unfinished Business — The Practical Side

"I'm not afraid to die. I just don't want to be there when it happens."
Woody Allen

The more unfinished business that can be taken care of during "early old age" the better. At any stage, the more family participation, in preparing to "finish" unfinished business, the better. This is especially true when it comes to legal documents such as wills and trusts (discussed in Chapter 6). Even when a carefully developed will and trust are "in order," there is one final document to complete which is called a "Letter of Instruction."

A *letter of instruction* is a guide to make it easier for a family to close out the affairs of the departing person. Although not a legal document, such a letter should be in agreement with the will. Senior family members may need or desire encouragement and specific help to complete a

173

letter of instruction. This may involve first, second, or even third level intervention. When required, the adult child should not hesitate to step in.

The suggestions beginning on page 176 are designed to help initiate a letter of instruction. They are presented in a worksheet format to encourage early completion.

BITS AND PIECES

Sometimes an older person will receive a "scare" from her or his doctor. This can motivate that person to quickly take care of some unfinished business. I once knew a 60 year old woman who learned one morning she needed major surgery the following day. That afternoon she purchased a new car and drove it around until late that night. Most of us should be able to deal with unfinished business without such a push. Check the items below that should be on your agenda.

☐ Taking your "dream trip" — to Rome, Paris, Hawaii — or a trip "home" with the right companion alongside.

☐ Completing the "family tree" that you started years ago.

☐ Writing your memoirs — perhaps with the help of a family member.*

☐ Re-doing the family albums.

☐ Taking a special trip with a grandchild.

☐ Planning a surprise birthday party for yourself, and inviting others you want to see.

☐ Renewing contact with old friends and arranging to visit them.

☐ Presenting treasured personal items to special people in your life under surprise circumstances.

---

* You may consider ordering a wonderful book titled *Changing Memories into Memoirs* by Fanny-Maude Evans. Write Crisp Publications, Inc., 95 First Street, Los Altos, CA 94022 for more information.

☐   Preparing and presenting a special "memory show"
     with slides and photos taken years earlier.

☐   Making a special gift to your favorite charity, organiza-
     tion or person.

ADD YOUR OWN: _____

_____

_____

_____

_____

_____

_____

_____

_____

_____

_____

_____

_____

THE LETTER OF INSTRUCTION

People to be Notified. Family members, close personal friends, professional people (lawyer, tax specialists), Social Security personnel, insurance agents, and other agencies need to be informed when the death of a family member takes place. It is best to prepare a list ahead of time. Sometimes such a list is many pages long. Telephone numbers and other data should be included. It often falls on a single family member or friend to see that such a list is completed and maintained. It can be a big job, so it is a good idea to start as soon as possible:

Names	Telephone #	Address

THE LETTER OF INSTRUCTION (cont.)

Names	Telephone #	Address

THE LETTER OF INSTRUCTION (cont.)

Disposal of Personal Possessions. Some senior family members prefer to dispose of furniture, jewelry, heirlooms, automobiles and other personal possessions as they grow older. They enjoy the special giving process as they go. Others prefer to list their possessions and have them distributed after they have "taken the ferry" (as my grandmother used to say). Even if 90% of possessions are distributed ahead of time, the others should be listed to prevent misunderstandings or hard feelings.

Item	*Recipient*
_____	_____
_____	_____
_____	_____
_____	_____
_____	_____
_____	_____
_____	_____
_____	_____
_____	_____
_____	_____
_____	_____
_____	_____

THE LETTER OF INSTRUCTION (cont.)

Item   *Recipient*

_____

_____

_____

_____

_____

_____

_____

_____

_____

_____

_____

_____

_____

_____

_____

_____

_____

THE LETTER OF INSTRUCTION (cont.)

Previous Promises. Any verbal promises made in the past by an aging family member, but never recorded, should be formalized and listed. This is best accomplished through discussion with a trusted family member. To avoid injured relationships later, such promises should be listed and signed by the senior family member. This is a sensitive area that can often cause misunderstandings.

_____

_____

_____

_____

_____

_____

_____

_____

_____

_____

_____

_____

_____

THE LETTER OF INSTRUCTION (cont.)

Miscellaneous. The following specific information needs to be recorded (location, addresses, other pertinent data).

Bank accounts _____

_____

_____

Credit cards _____

_____

_____

Deeds _____

_____

_____

Mortgages _____

_____

_____

Safe Deposit Box (include location of key and list of contents) _____

_____

_____

_____

THE LETTER OF INSTRUCTION (cont.)

Money owed by others _____

_____

_____

Money owed to others _____

_____

_____

Prior tax returns and current tax file _____

_____

_____

Insurance policies _____

_____

_____

Survivor benefits _____

_____

_____

Other data:* _____

_____

_____

* See Appendix (page 223) for Funeral Arrangements Guide to be attached to the Letter of Instruction.

THE LETTER OF INSTRUCTION (cont.)

Right To Die Declaration. Such a notice can often be a simple letter or note which states the individual does not wish to have artificial means employed to extend life when life is nearing completion (medically authenticated). The note should contain location, date, signature of the individual and should be signed by two witnesses. Some states have a formal form called *Durable Power of Attorney for Health Care Decisions.* It is a good idea to check with your lawyer to insure this declaration (if desired) is in compliance with the law.

Other: _____

_____

_____

_____

_____

_____

_____

_____

_____

_____

Note: If death occurs before a letter of instruction has been completed, the above guide may help an executor of the will (in cooperation with other family members) to help "finish unfinished business."

GIVING AN ATTORNEY THE POWER TO ACT FOR THE FAMILY

It is always possible that a senior family member may wind up without the mental ability to make decisions for his or her own well-being. (Alzheimer's disease, for example, takes a tragic toll on a number of older people). In some cases, the final unfinished business can be turned over to a trusted individual (family or non-family member), and the involvement of an attorney is not necessary. In other cases — especially when there is a sizable estate and little agreement among heirs — finding the right attorney and empowering him/her to act can be in the best interest of everyone concerned.

A *Power Of Attorney* document transfers the power of decision-making to a designated person. This must occur while the senior is still sufficiently competent to know what she or he is doing. Powers transferred can be extremely broad — and cover everything from major financial and estate problems to the kind of care the senior will receive.

Because a power of attorney can grant authority to dispose, sell, and encumber real and personal property, extreme caution should be used. Unless otherwise designated, such powers are indefinite. Thus, the right to revoke a *Power Of Attorney* can sometimes be critical to the welfare of the family.

A standard *Power Of Attorney* form can usually be purchased at a local stationery store. Should you obtain one, you will notice that the document needs to be signed and stamped by a Notary Public and recorded. For these, and many other reasons, it is always a good idea to consult a lawyer before seeking to make such a drastic move.

It is also wise to consider the use of a *Power Of Attorney* between spouses so that when one is left in charge, she or he has the power to make the decisions. In this instance, the process is less complicated, but consulting a lawyer, may still be wise.

ONE STEP AWAY

Often the adult child of a dying parent is too emotionally involved to deal effectively with the loss. Normal common sense can give way to grief. When this happens, it is best for someone else (i.e. a spouse or close friend) to take charge. The trauma is less when such an individual is in control. Objectivity is more likely.

> When Marcy lost her mother she was unable to deal with the decisions that needed to be made quickly. Her good friend and neighbor, Jeff, had no trouble assuming this responsibility. His greater detachment made it possible.
>
> When Mrs. Franks lost her devoted husband, she and her adult children were stunned to the point they could do little but console each other. Solution? The spouses of her children (one step away) took over. Fortunately, a Letter of Instruction prepared earlier acted as a guide to the unfinished business at hand.

An individual one step away can be more objective. This person can communicate with others more easily, and if necessary, make the hard decisions that need to be made.

SUMMARY
1. Once a will (and possibly a trust) is in order, completing a Letter of Instruction is necessary to wind up the practical side of unfinished business.

2. A Letter of Instruction should be completed in the presence of the senior family member with as much family involvement as possible.

3. In some cases, giving an attorney the power to act for a family deserves deep consideration.

THE FAMILY NEXT DOOR

This is a simple story that actually happened to a friend of mine. Mabel lost her husband 15 years ago. Thanks to the daily support provided by a younger family next door, she survived gracefully in her own home until very recently. The family next door really cared about Mabel. She would raise a certain blind each morning to signal that all was well. Taking a lunch or dinner to Mabel's house was not uncommon. (Mabel learned to love tacos, enchiladas, and other Mexican dishes). Whenever Mabel needed to visit a doctor or go shopping, she could count on her neighbors for a car and driver.

Mabel had a daughter and granddaughter who *could* have provided the love and support that came from the family next door. Such help was seldom forthcoming.

The story ended on a happy note (at least for the family next door). Mabel left her lovely home to them as a sign of her deep appreciation. The family did what they did for Mabel simply out of love and concern; and had no expectation of any rewards. Mabel demonstrated she was still in charge until the end.

FAMILY STUDY #25 **Mrs. Alder's Label Party Idea**

Mrs. Alder is a delight. In a social setting, she is vibrant and totally in command. A widow, Mrs. Alder is somewhere in her eighties. At the present time she lives alone in a lovely home with a live-in maid. She recently made the decision to move into a life-care facility within her financial "comfort zone."

Mrs. Alder and her husband did a great deal of traveling in their younger years. As a result, they accumulated many valuable pieces of art. In making the decision to move, her number one problem was what to do with her treasured possessions. She finally decided to divide them evenly among her three sons. At the advice of her lawyer, she started to prepare a letter of instruction to go with her will.

The letter covered such matters as the funeral arrangements, people to notify, etc. An important part of the letter was a list of who should receive each possession. Shortly after starting the list, Mrs. Alder became discouraged. How could she be fair? How could she please everyone? One son and his spouse might appreciate one item, while another son and spouse could prefer something else.

She finally decided it would be more fun to throw a "label" party. This would let her children figure things out for themselves. The idea would be to invite everyone for a weekend — children and grandchildren. She would plan a special outing for the grandchildren so her adult children would be free. She would then present each member with a list of the possessions and their appraised values. Each family would also be given a supply of labels. Then, they would select those possessions they preferred. Negotiations could take place and decisions would be made. Once a decision had been made, a label would be attached to the article with the name of one son on it.

When Mrs. Alder returned with the grandchildren, the labels would be attached, and the distribution of her possessions would be complete. All she would need to do is locate labels and make a list for later distribution.

What flaws do you see in the label system? Mrs. Alder wants to bring her family closer together. Will this approach accomplish this goal?

Place a check in the appropriate square below and then give your reasons for your choice in the spaces provided.

☐   I believe Mrs. Alder should complete the letter of instruction by herself. My reasons are:

_____

_____

_____

_____

☐   I vote for the "label party" for the following reasons:

_____

_____

_____

To compare your answer with that of the authors, please turn to page 213.

FAMILY STUDY #26   **Let's Talk About It Later**

The toughest thing Mike, Matt, and Marge ever had to do was meet their mother at the airport and tell her that her youngest son, Mel, had just been killed in a boating accident. Upon hearing the news, their mother went into shock. Even after six months, she cannot talk about the tragedy.

On top of the emotional adjustment for the family, legal changes needed to be made to the will and living trust. Also, a Letter of Instruction has never been prepared. Mel's mother (now in her mid-eighties) is so depressed that every time legal matters are mentioned she says, "Let's talk about that later."

How long should the children wait? When, (if at all), should they proceed on their own? What would you recommend to Mike, Matt, and Marge? Write out your answer and then review the views found on page 213.

_____

_____

_____

_____

_____

14

Finishing Unfinished Business — The Emotional Side

"I remember those happy days and often wish I could speak into the ears of the dead the gratitude which was due to them in life and so ill-returned."
Gwyn Thomas

Paying a final compliment and communicating love is as much a part of unfinished business as preparing a Letter of Instruction. It is often easier to compliment children on their swimming skills than say something nice about the way a senior gets around with a cane after a stroke. It is easier to compliment a student with good grades than give deserved recognition to a parent who may have survived a serious illness. It is easier to praise adult children on a business success than to tell an aging parent that he or she is an inspiration to others. Seniors deserve compliments as much as, or more than those younger, and often need them more.

189

This is especially true when time is short. The emotional finality of paying a personal compliment or providing a farewell expression of love is often so difficult many people never get around to it.

A GREATER NEED FOR COPING MECHANISMS

Coping is a process of dealing with difficult problems without putting undue pressure on your emotional and mental health. A *mechanism* is a technique that helps make successful coping possible. These mechanisms can be thought of as "safety valves." They can permit a person to release inner tensions harmlessly. An example of a healthy mechanism (safety valve) is when a problem is shared with a friend or family member.

Some mechanisms are naturally built-in to most personalities. For example, shedding tears will help most people express and release feelings harmlessly. Some mechanisms, however, need to be *developed*. Properly done, they can prevent over-reacting to a situation.

TOO CLOSE FOR COMMUNICATION?

My observations indicate that the more intense the love between a child and parent, the more difficult it may be to verbally communicate these emotions.

> Paul and his father never had any trouble communicating about boating, fishing, and other casual matters. In fact, friends commented that Paul and his father were unusually close. But for 40 years their conversations dealt only with surface matters. Although the need was there, neither party was able to introduce subjects concerned with love, death, or family conflicts.

Why do we find this situation between individuals who obviously love each other? The following observations are raised for your consideration.

1. Does love somehow form its own communication block? Do love and respect run so deeply within some people that they cannot find words to match their feelings, and thereby say nothing?

2. Is fear at the bottom of the communication block? Are some parents viewed as authority figures making adult children afraid to embarrass themselves by openly expressing their love? Are there individuals who can express love to others but not their parents?

3. Is there a false premise involved in the inability to communicate? Do adult children and parents tell themselves that actions speak more loudly than words?

Whatever the cause, this communications block often makes it impossible to complete the emotional side of unfinished business. Although difficult for some, three possible solutions are suggested. The first is to force communication by saying that love has been so deep it has been impossible to talk about. A second thought is to write a special message and read it to the individual. A third possibility would be to write a letter that expresses your feelings and leave it for the person you cannot verbally embrace. Sometimes, a heartfelt letter will pave the way for verbal communication.

When accomplished in time, little in the realm of unfinished business can be more significant to both parties than an expression of love. The family member preparing to depart this life can read and re-read the letter prior to their peaceful journey. The remaining person can eliminate the possibility of later regrets if he or she can somehow communicate the words "I love you."

PUTTING RELATIONSHIPS IN ORDER

Restoring broken relationships is something that should take place throughout life. But no matter how successful a person might be at this process, there are always some loose ends that need to be resolved as a part of unfinished business. Most departing family members want to leave with a "clean slate." Those remaining normally wish to "get things off their chest" in order to dissipate later guilt feelings.

Even in the best of situations, repairing relationships is awkward and difficult. Often, damaged relationships that could have been restored, are never improved. When a person is young, it often seems easier to replace a broken relationship than repair it. Even when a senior family member may not have much time, some seem to prefer "passing" on their "last chance" when they could reconcile differences. When this happens, unfinished business remains.

THE ABILITY TO EXPRESS EMOTIONS

An ability to experience and express emotions is uniquely human. Emotion is that part of us that contributes to feelings of great joy or great sorrow, and permits us to receive and express love.

Most people grieve when a loved one dies. These feelings are normal, and when experienced fully, they allow a person to adapt to the loss. If these feelings are not dealt with satisfactorily, despair may occur. Instead of being able to work through the sense of pain and loss, a person's depression can become chronic and incapacitating.

Expressing your emotions openly when you lose a special person is healthy and good. Understanding these emotions and learning how to express them is the sign of a mature person.

UNFINISHED COMMUNICATIONS EXERCISE

Final meetings with a dying family member or friend are never easy. Anxiety, uncertainty and the fear of saying the wrong thing are present. Following are four possible approaches to such a meeting. Read and answer the questions on the following pages.

1. **The Pollyanna Approach:** Although the medical facts (and observation) say differently, advocates of this approach say things like, "You will be up and around in no time". These individuals are coping the best way they know, but they should realize that such comments may keep the other party from being able to speak openly about dying. It can add a burden to the dying person because of a compulsion to sustain the falseness of the situation.

2. **A Reflective Approach:** Some find it safe to simply discuss the beautiful parts of the past and ignore the present. These individuals believe that discussing the past will give the individual some pleasure, and perhaps additional strength and confidence. Although the reflective approach can be comforting, it may close communication for discussing more serious matters that could benefit both parties.

3. **An Accept and Discuss Approach:** Although often difficult to get started, this approach will give an individual a chance to "open up" and say things they may wish to say before it is too late. Discussing death can be the kind of spiritual experience that is most needed. Next to prayer itself, accepting and discussing the inevitable is often the best therapy.

    To start such a discussion, certain questions may need to be asked, such as, "Are there some things you want to discuss at this stage of your illness? Are you worried about the future like I am?"

4. **The Wait and Listen Approach:** Some visitors prefer to wait about initiating a conversation with a dying person. These individuals often start by holding the patient's hand and just waiting. They seem to feel the less they say at the start the better. This is often a valid approach. A very ill person generally will let others know when she or he is facing death. Their conversation is often a signal because they say things like: "I don't seem to be getting any better, do I?", or "We've had a good life together," or, "We've enjoyed some good times, haven't we?"

Questions:

1. Which of the four approaches fits best into your own comfort zone? _____

    _____

2. Which approach do you feel will do the most for the family member of friend? _____

    _____

3. Which approach would be better if children are present?

    _____

4. Which would leave you (as the visitor) feeling best about your visit? _____

    _____

Based upon the information presented above, write the approach you would use in visiting a loved one, perhaps for the last time.

_____

_____

_____

_____

_____

_____

_____

_____

SPIRITUAL MATURITY

Like the ocean tides, life seems to surge and fall at regular intervals. Sometimes giant waves of creativity burst upon the barren sand followed by a period of great calm.

It is comfortable but misleading to think of the last stage of life as a time to withdraw from reality and flow quietly to sea. Of course, our body energy fades and often asks for rest, but this need not happen to our minds. Tides of creativity can continue to ebb and flow within our minds. We should never foolishly try to stop it. We need stormy episodes to exercise and tax our minds even when our body cannot keep pace. We need to move fearlessly into new corridors of spiritual growth even if we are physically stranded. Our bodies may slow years before we are ready to cross Tennyson's "Bar"; but our minds can continue to ebb and flow.

Exploring the spiritual challenges of life should continue until the final ebbtide. The concluding surge should be a crescendo of joy and understanding. That is what spiritual maturity is all about.

THE THREE R'S The more unfinished business that has been concluded, the easier it will be for those left behind. Still, no one is fully prepared when death arrives.

On the positive side, nothing seems to bring a family circle closer together — if only for a time — than the loss of a member. Strange as it may seem, the closer the relationship has been, the greater the opportunity for future benefits. Perhaps this is because an individual will search more deeply for his or her personal spirituality. Although each family member and friend will interpret his or her loss in a unique way, the "Three R's" approach Release, Remember and Renew, may be helpful.

Release: The word heard most often is *Release*. It is often mutually rewarding. The dying family member may have been in pain or uncomfortable circumstances long enough. Some key family members may have shouldered a difficult responsibility long enough. To all parties, release can be beautiful.

Remember: The deceased has left untold memories in the minds of those remaining. With generous selectivity, the beautiful memories should be remembered and kept alive within the family circle. Many memories will become a part of "family lore." The more these "stories" are passed along to other members, the more unity the family circle will have in the future. Photographs and family albums can play an important part in such transmissions. Not everyone can leave something for society to remember. With a little effort, however, everyone can leave something for a family to remember. This is a significant legacy!

Renew: The loss of a family member should eventually convert into a positive, enriching experience. In a psychological sense, the strength of the lost member is distributed among those remaining. This is often manifested when a sibling or grandchild dedicates him or herself to launch a personal renewal effort. Somehow the experience can identify and restore important values that otherwise might have been lost.

SUMMARY

1. Paying final compliments and verbalizing expressions of love is so difficult for some people that they choose instead to do it by letter.

2. It is as important to pay final compliments and transmit expressions of love as it is to take care of the practical side of unfinished business.

3. The Three R's emphasize that those who have built and enjoyed strong, loving relationships can often gain the most from the loss of a senior family member.

FAMILY STUDY #27   **Family Intervention?**

All members of the Jackson family anticipate a call any day that their mother has taken her own life. Two of the four children are reconciled over the possibility and feel that their mother has the right to take such action without interference from anyone. The remaining three want to take some kind of preventive action before it is too late.

Mother Jackson lives alone under comfortable financial circumstances. She has been dealing magnificently with cancer for six years, but has recently become increasingly depressed over her impossible condition. Whenever she and her doctor start to feel there is a spark of hope, the cancer shows up in a different location. Although she has accepted various forms of counseling and group therapy in the past, she now refuses help of any kind. Slowly, in quiet conversations with her children, she has prepared them for the possibility. Her favorite expression is, "Life has been good to me and I would prefer to bow out with as little trouble to others and pain to myself as possible. Your father and I talked this over before I lost him. He would understand and I hope you might also. It is the only way I will find peace."

What action, if any, do you feel the family should take? Write out your answer below and then turn to page 214.

FAMILY STUDY #28   Charlie

Charlie is a deeply loved father and grandfather. A gentle man, almost everyone at one time or another has come to Charlie with their problems. They always seemed to leave with a greater sense of self-worth. Up until a short time ago, Charlie's greatest joy in life was spending time with his grandchildren.

A few weeks ago, Charlie was admitted to a nursing home because of a diagnosed case of Alzheimer's disease. A few days after being admitted, Charlie wandered away from the facility and was found blocks away unable to account for his actions.

After this incident, the family doctor and nursing home manager had a serious talk with Charlie's daughter and son. "Your father has moved into a level of dementia from which there is probably no return. There is no cure. He will require close observation. Controls, including straps, may be necessary. We thought you should know so that you and other members of the family can start to adjust. One thing you can feel good about is that your mother is not here to go through this with Charlie."

Charlie's daughter and son left the nursing home in such a despondent state that they decided to discuss the matter over several drinks. The daughter said, "When your mind goes first you are dead before you die." The son replied, "Yeah, it is going to be a double death for Dad. I'm not sure that I can cope, but what worries me most are our kids. You know how much they love him. Should we protect them from what has happened?"

If you were Charlie's daughter or son, what would you do? What would Charlie want? Is it best for the grandchildren to see and know Charlie in this state? How can they protect themselves? Write out your answer and then compare them with those on page 215.

_____

_____

_____

_____

Suggested Answers
To Family Studies

The *Family Studies* at the end of each chapter were designed to present "real world" situations to help prepare the reader for what may lie ahead. Please use the interpretations provided here as a guide to your own thinking. There are no "correct" answers. Different points of view are expected and should be discussed. New insights can develop when alternative points of view are expressed and discussed.

1. **Jerome's Dilemma:** Although options 1, 2, and 3 are sound immediate steps, now might be a good time for Jerome to take his family to Oklahoma for a visit. Instead of trusting luck (option 4) or stalling (option 6), Jerome could use his father's "driving problem" as an opportunity to pull the family closer together to help prepare for future unfinished business. Such a visit could also enhance the pending golden wedding anniversary; give Jerome's children a chance to know their grandparents better and allow for an evaluation of medical facts. It will also encourage communication among family members and better define future leadership roles.

2. **Sylvia Blows Her Top:** Sylvia should be complimented for taking such a strong position. Many adult children underestimate the capacity of their parents to care for themselves. It is a mistake to provide support before it is really needed. With this in mind, the following thoughts might be helpful:

    1. Adult children are not the owners of their parents' lives. Having parents reach an advanced age is not a cue to begin determining what is good for them.

2. It is important to build good parental relationships throughout adulthood in order to better appreciate our parents, and admire the graceful adaptations aging induces. A sharing relationship will not create a sudden time when we begin to think, "What will we do with mother?" This discussion will have started much earlier and the options will have been built into the relationship. This doesn't mean things will be easy but there will be a sensitivity to what parents of adult children want and need.

3. The best solution to parental aging is not intervention by adult children, but an assurance that the children are there, are aware, and willing to be of assistance. When "taking over" becomes necessary, it should be done with loving reluctance and alertness to the possibility of returning powers to an aging parent whenever possible.

4. Adult children need to remember that their parents will always retain their parental roles. They never, even when senile, become children.

5. In dealing with aging parents, adult children need to keep growing and developing. Aging parents do not want their children to penalize themselves because of excessive care. No matter how much attention a parent needs, a portion of time must be reserved for the caring child.

3. **Communication Opportunities For Gary:** *(Part I)* It is too much to expect Gary to turn into a good communicator overnight, even if he wants to change. It seems reasonable that Gary will start talking with Hilda and then exercise option 1 and 2. It is possible he might apologize to his sister. Even later, Gary might initiate a family meeting. If he does this, he will contribute to the cohesiveness of the family and make things easier for Hilda. This will help Gary eliminate his guilts.

(Part 2) Perhaps Gary will begin to visit his father and mother more frequently. He could also make an effort to see other family members more often. These actions would signal love and concern even when Gary cannot communicate love verbally. With the help of Hilda, Gary might write down his feelings. Everyone would benefit if Gary would be willing to attend a suitable support group with Hilda.

4. **Which Letter Should Mrs. Snow Send?:** Letter number 2 (family reunion) stands the best chance of correcting what appears to be a "reward imbalance" between Mrs. Snow and her brothers. Mrs. Snow deserves recognition, appreciation, and love from her brothers. Until they understand first hand the problems she faces, and the level of care she is providing, her brothers will not give her the recognition she deserves.

    With letter number 1, the brothers could offer financial help, and show greater concern from a distance. This will not bring the families together in a reunion. Sending money and showing concern from a distance is one thing, making arrangements for a family reunion is another. Mrs. Snow's mother needs to see her sons and they need to see her. They may also be ignoring how important it is for their children to know their grandmother.

    Once Mrs. Snow sends the "reunion" letter, she should make follow-up calls to arrange the best possible dates, and continue to communicate regularly about the condition of her mother.

5. **Reverse Abuse:** This case highlights how past relationships affect the way we often deal with aging parents. It would seem that Maria has not accepted the fact that her mother has never liked her as well as her brother. Maria has tried to win her mother's love by being a rug under the mother's feet. Maria has a great deal of unfinished business.

As a support group moderator, it would be vital to get Maria to understand her situation in order to free herself from the desperate need to gain her mother's approval. She may ultimately have to accept the fact that her mother will never give that approval. The key for Maria is to understand that the withholding of approval by her mother has nothing to do with Maria's worth. She can learn to be a successful happy person without it.

Maria must begin doing things for her mother because she wants to do them, not because she is pressured to do them. Once this has been achieved, the rebuffs will be easier to bear. It is possible she should start doing less. This alone could help turn the relationship around.

One thing Maria can do immediately is to stop any "war" from escalating. She can do this by leaving and returning when things are more reasonable. She can also make clear that she will not continue any conversation that is demeaning to her.

Helping Maria could be a real challenge. "Support" from other family members is essential.

6. **John And Heidi:** Heidi's idea is excellent and she should try to persuade John to attend based on the issues that will be addressed, and the "quality factor" normally present in such support groups. For example, the objection of "airing dirty linen in public" is handled in a professional manner and mistakes others may have made help those facing similar problems.

It is easy to build a positive case for support groups and seminars run by community aging agencies, churches, or temples. They can do much to help adult children handle current problems and prepare for the future. Some groups specialize in providing information and referrals. Some are discussion groups. Others do both, but all are worthwhile. Support groups allow families such as John and Heidi's to see that they are not alone, and the problems and concerns they have are not abnormal. Support groups can provide many fresh ideas about how to handle aging issues. These seminars help adult children determine which problems are relational and which are functional and what can be done about either. In addition, attending a support group may bring John and Heidi closer together as they face the unfinished business that lies ahead of them.

7. **Warren's Disturbing Condition:** From the limited data presented, it appears that both Warren Jr. and Sandy feel strong family ties to their father but neither has kept in very close contact recently. If this is the first time they have been willing to face the fact their father has a serious drinking problem, they should meet with their father to determine:

   (a) If their father will discuss his problem.

   (b) If he needs to see a doctor.

   (c) What local alcohol abuse programs are available, and whether Warren Sr. will agree to attend one.

   (d) If his medical insurance will cover the expenses.

   If Warren Sr. refuses to see a doctor, Warren Jr. and Sandy should continue their efforts until they decide if some form of intervention is required. Until then, Warren Sr.'s friends or neighbors should be alerted to make them aware. They could also try to help their father find some substitute activities.

   It would be a good idea for both Warren Jr. and Sandy to find counseling for themselves so they can deal with their feelings toward their father. Their goal should be to restore and improve relationships with their father. They should realize that it is up to their father to make sense and worth out of his own life, but they can be available for help.

8. **Communication Compatibility:** The author suggests that: (1) perhaps they can really communicate for the first time because both have a greater need and are taking time to listen; (2) the author feels it is one indication, but nothing more.

9. **Turnover:** The following steps are suggested:

Step 1: Let the entire matter ride for a few weeks to see if there is a change in the attitude of the mother. She may be over-reacting to the trauma of losing her husband, or there may be some hidden resentments to having been confined too much in the past. In either case, more time is required for the best decision.

Step 2: While staying in close contact with his mother and discussing her concerns openly, John should present the problem to his sisters. Their input is crucial and a family meeting would be desirable.

Step 3: Because turning things over so suddenly is uncharacteristic of his mother, John should point out why staying in charge could be best for her in the long run. A professional counselor might help provide an answer.

Step 4: A family meeting should be arranged so that the matter can be discussed openly from many directions. As a result of the meeting, John and his sisters should design a "turnover plan" that pleases their mother and protects the interests of the family.

Many senior family members tire of responsibility and want to be free. Widowhood often brings this to the surface. For many, however, the trauma of cutting the strings of authority loose is greater than they anticipate. As a result, some prematurely turn things over and then regret their actions later. The more the "turnover process" can be slowed the better, especially for John's mother.

10. **Can Of Worms:** The strategy of Mrs. Evers seems to offer the best promise of bringing the family closer together. This might occur if the distribution of the estate starts out slowly and is accompanied by some happy reunions or family vacations where relationships can be restored.

With a major effort, some of the estate could still be saved for distribution based upon the "Mutual Reward Theory" through a will. This might satisfy Mr. Evers and give the children more time to contribute to the emotional support of their parents.

11. **Mr. Monroe Upsets The Family:** The children should make every effort to support their father in enjoying his new relationship. There is currently no talk of marriage — and their fears of the misuse of his monies may be unfounded.

By supporting their father and welcoming his friend into the family circle, they will be able to determine if his new friend seems good for him. Even if they remain skeptical of the woman's designs, they should refrain from any comments regarding her intentions unless there is proof that she is trying to get his money.

If there is serious evidence that the woman is not being honest, this evidence should be well researched and then it would be appropriate for members of the family to try to talk to him about the designing woman.

The only concerns that the children rightfully should address would relate to his plans for his future for himself — not themselves. While parents are alive, children have no right to their (parents') property or monies. Inheritance monies are a gift, not a right.

If the relationship looks serious, the children might get legal advice for their father about written agreements that have been worked out for people in their situation. Once again, this should be for the father's interest, not the expected inheritance of the children.

12. **Mom's Decision:** Dorothy's mother appears to be fully capable of making her own decisions. If this is true, and she wants Dorothy to have the bulk of her estate, then her decision should be honored. Dorothy's mother, no doubt, has spent hours thinking over the matter and it may be her best way of showing her love and appreciation. In fact, as close as the two have been, neither party may be able to verbally express their love for each other.

    As far as dealing with the other children, a problem should not be anticipated. If, sometime in the future, Dorothy is left alone, she can "even things out" with what monies she receives from the estate. Right now it would appear that Dorothy will play the major support role as far as the unfinished business of her mother is concerned. Not knowing what might be ahead, Dorothy should accept the compliment without guilt feelings of any kind. And who knows, maybe it will take all of the estate money before her responsibility is over. Dorothy and the other children should continue to do what they do for their mother for love.

13. **What Is The Answer?** The situation is different for each aging person, so it is possible to defend both Mr. James and Mr. Wood. If Mr. James relaxes too much (and neglects his exercise program) he could start aging faster because there is truth to the expression, "use it or lose it." Mr. Wood, because of his feisty attitude, may stay more involved. So if he continues his exercise program he too could age more slowly. It is unfortunate, however, that Mr. Wood is unable to stay involved without turning people against him.

14. **Barbara Takes Over:** Many adult children take over doing things for their parents long before it is necessary. Even when parents are in care facilities, this type of over-protection continues. These adult children seem unable to find an approach that would let parents know assistance is available as they move toward the final stage of unfinished business.

Most parents appreciate *knowing* assistance is available, but prefer to do all they can for themselves as long as possible.

To some parents, too much family help is more embarrassing than getting more outside assistance. But even when outside help is the answer, adult children should let their parents know that they are ready to assist at any time. From time to time, it is a good idea for adult children to monitor parental reaction to the degree of assistance being provided. It is also a good idea to watch for signs of needless helplessness. It is important that older people do as much as they can, for as long as they can, even if it is awkward and incomplete.

Barbara should not be too hard on herself for doing what is natural to her — *taking over*. What she is doing is probably not a putdown to her father, but he is justified in requesting a stop to it. Barbara might list the things she is currently doing for her father and discuss which items he would like her to continue doing. She should let him know which give her pleasure.

Barbara may need to face the fact that her father won't receive some of the attention he is currently receiving when she pulls back, but he may be happier. This is because what he receives he will have achieved on his own.

15. **Too Much Of A Good Thing:** Ray is in a difficult situation. One approach would be for Ray to locate a support group for adult children having similar problems with their parents. Another approach would be for Ray and Janice to seek professional counseling. Either could help Janice sort out what is reasonable as far as caring for her parents. She needs to learn that "over-doing" can actually be harmful and might destroy the "balance" she needs in her own family.

It is also possible that Ray is experiencing some jealousy about his wife's divided attentions. It is to his credit that he is addressing these feelings openly. Ray needs to find ways in which he and Janice can do more things together. Perhaps Ray could contribute more to help Janice with her parents instead of sitting on the sidelines. Perhaps he needs to find other healthy outlets for his time so that he is not as dependent on Janice.

Any of the actions above should contribute to a better marriage between Ray and Janice.

16. **A Decision For The Parr Family:** A group meeting with the family minister and doctor present shows promise, providing Mrs. Parr is given full opportunity to express her fears and misgivings. Her pride should be respected. Giving examples of how personal friends have accepted assistance could help.

Option 2 also offers promise. Slowly getting used to one form of assistance at a time makes sense. As far as forcing Mrs. Parr to make a choice one way or another (option 1), restraint should be practiced. Of course, if Mrs. Parr raises the probability, the subject should be explored.

Fierce independence is a characteristic common among many older people. As achievers in a free country, they came by it honestly and the resistance they sometimes show may delay their aging. It is often a slow process for them to see the value of the Mutual Reward Theory relative to their own unfinished business. Open discussion appears to be the best possible approach to reach this goal.

17. **Reactions:** As Mrs. Johnson, I believe I would appreciate knowing that my children cared enough about me to construct a plan similar to the one described. It would motivate me to try harder and do more for myself. If I were Mr. Johnson, I think I would be more open (as he indicated) and start to feel much better about taking care of "the unfinished business" of my life. I would look forward to the family strategy meetings.

As John, Julie, or Christine I believe I would feel good about the strategy so long as my contribution did not take too much time away from my family and lifestyle. I would (as Julie mentioned) also want the experience to have some "fun" attached to it. My worry is that everyone could become too serious and over-involved. If this happens, the strategy would collapse because of human conflicts and everyone would go his or her separate way.

18. **Strengths/Weaknesses:** The author feels there are three major strengths: (1) parent/adult child involvement and communication is excellent and serves as the foundation of the strategy; both parents are attempting to do more for themselves which indicates the strategy is working; (2) the short-term aspects of the plan are sound, and long-term considerations are surfacing at the request of the parents; this is a healthy sign; (3) the fact that everyone lives close and meetings can be scheduled is a major advantage to keep the strategy in operation. The goal of maintaining the strategy without allowing it to become an excessive burden on any individual is a challenge that can be met only through frequent communications and adjustments.

    The three major weaknesses appear to be: (1) over-structuring, which could lead to the strategy becoming too much like business because there are not enough "fun times;" (2) too much change, too soon; with John, Julia, and Christine all showing so much interest (and making improvements) so soon, it could overwhelm Mr. and Mrs. Johnson; a slower pace might be easier to maintain; (3) over-promising—all three adult children volunteered to do so much at the start that they might not follow-through and resentments and conflicts could occur.

19. **Raymond Brings His Mother Home:** Raymond did things to his mother that he would never want done to himself — he decided what was good for her. In some way his mother must have felt he knew best because we are not told of any strong argument that she opposed the interventions he made in her life. Perhaps

she felt she had to please her only son because there would be no one else to care for, or about her, if he turned against her. Perhaps she was weary of trying everything on her own and welcomed the intervention, not knowing that it was not in her best interests.

Raymond's assumption that it was a good idea to move Mother in with them is naive and lacks depth. The best move Raymond could have made was to help his mother regain her control or find assistance in her own setting. It is almost always easier to heal and prosper in familiar surroundings with the friends we know around us. Adult children should "move Mother or Dad in with them" only with great caution and after first using all the resources within their parents and their own community.

Before any move away from familiar surroundings takes place, there should be serious attention given to the concept that the parent might be better off living in an adaptive setting in their own home area, rather than being moved to the children's home. It may seem more difficult for the adult children because they cannot control things, but that is just as well. Control should not be taken until it is either given or is absolutely necessary. Moves should not be made simply so adult children worry less.

When the move to the children's home is considered necessary, it should be a joint decision, and the ground for it should have been laid through many discussions over a period of time.

Adult children should realize that they cannot be the sole source of relationships to their aging parents when they "move them in," and many efforts should be made to help the older person develop her/his own network.

The older person will need to feel that they are making a contribution to the family, and the adult children need to see that this is a meaningful experience. This doesn't mean that the older persons are made caretakers of their children's family or that they need to make financial contributions (although this might be one solution); the family needs to discuss what its needs are and let the older person determine how they think they can help.

Families who have older members "move in" need to build in check points for their marital relationships and their own nuclear relationships. This means seeing to it that the nuclear family has a chance to review how the situation is working, speak about how it is affecting them, and seek help when someone seems to be experiencing difficulty. No one should be berated for finding it hard to have an older member of the family "move in," nor should it be a surprise that the older member might also find it hard to adjust.

20. **Solution For Ralph:** It is time for Ralph to force a decision to protect all parties involved, especially Martha. A combination of option 1, 2, and 3 may be best in this situation. Option 4 is not recommended. It would appear that Martha is unable to make a decision even with Ralph's support, so it is up to Ralph to take action. The best way to do this may be to bring other members of the family into the picture along with the family doctor and/or other professionals. All of the intervention signals appear clear. Only damage can be done through further delay.

21. **Mrs. Ames's Friend Hugo:** The Ames family should review the following before taking final action:

- Be sure that the problem could not be solved with live-in or temporary help for both Mrs. Ames and Hugo.

- Assure Mrs. Ames that the family will bring the dog to the nursing home for regular visits. As long as it is kept on a leash, it can be in the building and on the grounds.

- Help Mrs. Ames to see that she isn't able to give Hugo the care he needs because of her own illness, and that the dog she loves so much deserves good care.

- "Board" Hugo in a family home so that Mrs. Ames can see he is happy and cared for.

- Do a trial run of a couple weeks at a nursing home, with Hugo coming for visits. A nursing home with a house pet might be helpful.

If all else fails, Mrs. Ames must be shown how her refusal to leave the dog and go to a nursing home disturbs the family and is causing considerable worry.

22. **Katherine's Attitude:** The behavior Katherine is demonstrating is counter-productive to the best interests of her mother. First, she should not be making decisions her mother appears capable of making herself.

Second, Katherine is not helping her mother adjust to the fact that she will continue to need much of the help she is now receiving. Rather, she is perpetuating the concept that her mother is not really sick, not really old, and it is just a "phase" she is going through. This stance is guaranteed to make adjustment within the facility more difficult for her mother.

Third, Katherine is alienating staff and residents, and in so doing, may be turning the professional care-givers and residents against her mother. As Katherine returns to her own comfortable lifestyle, she leaves her mother with more to contend with, not less.

Katherine's mother needs all the support she can get. The recreational programs offered by the facility, the socializing between residents (especially those in similar condition and background), and the personal treatment of professionals will all make the situation better for her mother who, despite limitations, can still grow and develop as a person.

23. **Silent Victory:** The author sides with Joel. A Master Senior whose children are too busy or unable to communicate about significant matters is fortunate to find another to fill the void. Most are not so lucky. Both Joel and Genevieve lost much more than a part of their inheritance. They are just beginning to sense this.

24. **Regrets:** Sam is wrong. The remorse Genelle and Marty appear to have is genuine. They are recognizing that they missed an opportunity to learn more about their own spirituality and mortality. This knowledge could help them both now and ultimately as they face their own death. For Master Seniors, the late-late years are seldom a disaster.

25. **Mrs. Alder's Label Party Idea:** The idea shows promise, but if not conducted in an orderly way, it could do more harm than good. If properly planned, the risk may be worth taking. Mrs. Alder has the right to distribute her possessions in any manner she wishes. She does not need to seek prior approval of her three sons or their spouses. She should, however, design a plan that would gain their acceptance and enthusiasm. Procedures should be clear, well-communicated, and fair. A big advantage of the label idea is that it would take the responsibility away from Mrs. Alder, and increase communication within the family. She should make up her mind ahead of time to go along with the choices gracefully. This idea would work much better in some families than others.

26. **Let's Talk About It Later:** The good news in this tragic situation is that the three remaining siblings are working together as a team. As long as this continues, and they communicate openly and freely with each other, the legal problems can be worked out.

    To start with, it might be appropriate to bring in an attorney to discuss the possibility of a "memorial" for Mel. This would give everyone a chance to express their grief, and at the same time, open the door for other legal decisions. As far as the Letter of Instruction is concerned, it might be best to leave this up to the sibling that could handle it in the most sensitive manner. If either Mike, Matt, or Marge should volunteer (and the other two accept) then this could be the best solution. Whomever is chosen should receive the full support of the other two.

It is possible that going through the process of legal changes may contribute in a positive way to the healing that must eventually take place for all family members.

27. **Family Intervention:** It is normal for people who are seriously ill to talk about death, and in some cases, how to hasten it. These individuals will generally say that they don't want to be a bother to their loved ones. This may or may not be the real reason. A few people feel they have a right to end their lives, and no medical, spiritual, or family pressure can change their minds.

Talk of ending one's life can sometimes be a way of coming to terms with the terminal implications of a disease. It says that the person has reconciled to impending death, and wants to say goodbye. The Jackson family should allow their mother to talk about death and help her take care of all the unfinished personal business they feel needs attention. This may be all that is necessary, and may stop the talk about ending life. If they are disturbed about her talk of ending her life, they should let her know how they feel.

It is important to surround the mother with all the supports that have been a natural part of her coping mechanisms over the years — her church, temple, etc.

Her talk about ending her life may just be that she is unwilling to take any more treatments for her disease. That is an unusual, but legitimate, decision and will need support from all the family.

If there is talk about actively hastening death, the family should discuss this with their physician. There may be a depression which is a natural outcome of so many assaults to the body, and there are clinical interventions that can be made to alleviate this.

There are legal implications to both giving the patient the means to end their lives, and not alerting authorities when it seems that it might happen. In the end, a person's life is theirs. A family that supports their loved one in every way will have no guilts when death does come to claim them.

28. **Charlie:** The unfinished business connected with Charlie will be most difficult for the family to face. The following suggestions, made in general terms, are designed to be as supportive as possible.

  a. Charlie's children could benefit from joining an Alheimer's support group (if one is available locally) so they can learn more about the disease and suitable coping mechanisms.

  b. Family members should keep in mind that Charlie can respond to warmth and tenderness even though he may not be able to respond coherently.

  c. It is almost always harmful to keep comparing a deteriorating person to the individual they used to be. In a sense, they are not the same person.

  d. Families can handle the "not recognizing" phase by gently saying who they are and the relationship between them.

  e. It may be best not to try to "force" the loved one to remember. They are not trying to make others miserable, the disease has simply caused their memory to become non-functional.

  f. There is rarely any good achieved by shielding other family members. The extent to which we must go to keep people from knowing and experiencing the truth, usually ends up being as hurtful as knowing from the start. Even grandchildren should know that their grandfather is ill and that his memories are slipping away. They should also understand that things are likely to get worse. How much they should know depends upon their age.

  g. It is important that adult children share their sadness, worries, and fears with their own children. When realities are discussed openly, we begin the healing process; when we have others we love to walk beside us, we heal that much faster.

APPENDIX
Funeral Arrangement Guide

This material has been prepared to assist senior family members to design their funeral service. It can be completed alone, or as a team project with selected family members, close friends, or professional caregivers. Most individuals will want to complete this guide *before* contacting the funeral home of their choice. This facilitates arrangements when death occurs and insures that the deceased's wishes are honored. Advance preparation also assists funeral directors and eases the burden on remaining family members. The completed funeral arrangement guide can be incorporated as part of a Letter of Instruction to accompany a will.

Trained funeral home representatives are available to provide professional guidance at any stage of preparation. When contact is made with a representative from a funeral home, it is suggested that the individual be viewed as any professional (such as doctor, lawyer, minister, or insurance agent). A well chosen individual can be invaluable in assisting family members conclude the final stages of unfinished business.

Beginning Exercise

The exercise on the following page is designed to prepare you for the material that follows. Answer the questions true or false and then match your answers with those provided at the end of the exercise.

	TRUE	FALSE
1. An individual has the right to design his or her own funeral service.	_____	_____
2. When it comes to funerals, more advance planning is taking place today.	_____	_____
3. A body can be cremated and still have a traditional or memorial service.	_____	_____
4. When a family plans a cremation following a traditional service, a casket can be rented from most funeral homes.	_____	_____
5. A typical funeral home can make arrangements for cremation and/or burial at sea.	_____	_____
6. Pre-need financial plans (i.e., paying the full costs of a prescribed funeral in advance) are more popular today.	_____	_____
7. In most states, if one specifies their wishes in advance, it becomes the duty of survivors to follow such wishes.	_____	_____
8. A mortician should be viewed as a respected counselor who is available 24 hours each day.	_____	_____
9. There are three legal ways to dispose of a body: (1) ground burial, (2) entombment in a mausoleum, (3) cremation.	_____	_____
10. When preparing a funeral for oneself, concern for those remaining should be given careful consideration.	_____	_____

ANSWERS: *All of the answers are true.*

Carefully read the material below. Topics covered include: Options Available, Expense Factors, and Pre-Need Funeral Contracts.

Here are things to consider when making decisions about funeral arrangements.

Options Available

Similar to wedding arrangements, a funeral service can have unlimited variations. Consider the following possibilities:

- A traditional funeral with a viewing period, formal service, and graveside committal.

- A traditional funeral without a viewing period or graveside service, or both.

- A private graveside service followed by a memorial.

- Immediate burial.

- Cremation only.

- Cremation with a memorial service.

- Cremation with a private service where the urn is committed to a mausoleum.

- Cremation with a formal service and a short service when the urn is placed in a mausoleum niche.

- Cremation with burial at sea.

- Add your own variations:

_____

_____

_____

_____

_____

Each individual and/or family needs to determine which type of funeral fits best into a personal "comfort zone." Keep options in mind as you read the next two sections. You will be invited to make choices at the end of this guide.

Expense Factors

As is true with weddings and other celebrations, designing a funeral service has expense factors which must be considered. Such expenses fall into four categories:

1. *Fees for services provided by funeral home.* These costs depend on the funeral home selected and the degree of their involvement. Picking up a body within a community and delivering it to a crematorium is a minimum involvement; embalming and a long list of other services (including unusual costs in the movement of a body long distances) could be maximum involvement. A funeral home will be able to provide you with a printed price list for all available services. Normally, there is a basic charge and you can select specific additional services.*

2. *Cost of Merchandise.* Caskets and urns can range from a few hundred dollars to several thousand dollars.

3. *Disposition of body.* Cemetery burial plots can range from a few hundred dollars to over a thousand. Mausoleum crypts often cost over a thousand dollars. Cremation is usually the least expensive.

4. *Miscellaneous expenses.* These expenses include payments to ministers, soloists, and those who provide motor escorts. Flowers may also be ordered through funeral homes. There is usually a small charge for Death Certificates.

* Under Federal Trade Commission rules, every funeral home is required to provide the consumer with an itemized list of charges for services, facilities, and equipment.

All expenses should be discussed thoroughly with a funeral home representative before selection. One should not hesitate to ask questions. For example, when selecting a casket, questions concerning these items are appropriate: description of the quality of construction, thickness of the casket wall, protection provided, reputation of manufacturer, etc.

Pre-need Funeral Contracts

Surveys indicate that about 90% of adults understand that pre-paid funeral plans are available. Yet it is estimated that only about 20% actually engage in such contracts.

The benefits of a pre-need contract include: (1) greater peace of mind because another piece of unfinished business has been handled in advance; (2) the kind of service desired has been guaranteed by a contract so that unexpected changes should not occur; (3) paid contracts do not burden remaining family members financially; (4) fewer decisions need be made at an emotional time for remaining family members and close friends. There are two types of basic pre-funeral contracts.

Funded. A growing number of people are deciding to fund their funeral expenses ahead of time. There are two common ways of doing this.

1. *Insurance Policy.* Many insurance companies offer a variety of plans. Once the details and expenses involved in a funeral have been determined, a policy can be written to pay the exact amount, which the funeral home will honor without any increases when the services are provided. Such a policy can be purchased through a funeral home or independently. Ask a funeral home representative for further details.

2. *Savings Trust.* Once the full cost of a predetermined funeral has been reached, the correct amount of money can be deposited in a savings account with the funeral home named as beneficiary. The interest that accumulates should off-set most inflationary increases.

Not Funded. Arrangements have been completed but funding is delayed until time of services. Many prefer to use their life insurance policies for this purpose. Others designate funds from other sources.

In either case, the insurance policy or savings account to pay for funeral services (along with complete funeral plans) can be on file in a predetermined place for the family and the mortuary.

With the information presented thus far, it should be possible for the reader to design his or her own funeral service. You are invited to complete the following form for your own satisfaction or for that of your family, and as an aid to a funeral home.

MY FUNERAL PREFERENCES
(Important Personal Data Included)

This form is designed to assist the funeral home of your choice. Do not feel compelled to complete the form in full. It is only a guide. Keep in mind that you may make it unnecessarily difficult for your family if you attempt to provide too much guidance.

Preliminary Data

1. The following persons are key members of my family and/or close friends. All should be notified of my death as soon as possible.

_____

_____

_____

_____

_____

_____

My clergyman is _____ Phone: _____

My physician is _____ Phone: _____

My lawyer is _____ Phone: _____

My insurance agent is _____ Phone: _____

My funeral director or home is:

    Name _____

    Address _____

    Telephone Number _____

MY FUNERAL PREFERENCES (cont.)

2. The following personal data is necessary for official certification. Accuracy is important. Claims, benefits, and legal procedures are involved.

Full Name:

_____

              first   *middle*   *last*

Current/last Residence:

_____

    street   *city*   *county*   *state*

Birthdate: _____ Birthplace: _____

Employer: _____ Retired? _____

Spouse: _____ Birthplace: _____
        (full maiden name)

Father: _____ Birthplace: _____
        (full name)

Mother: _____ Birthplace: _____
        (full maiden name)

Social Security Number:* _____

If ever employed by a railroad, list company and dates: _____

_____

If ever in Armed Services, Service Serial Number: _____

* Upon your death, the Social Security Administration should be notified immediately (the telephone number can be found under Health and Human Services in the United States Government Offices section in the front part of a telephone directory). When there is a remaining spouse or dependent child, as of 1987, a $255.00 death benefit is payable. A Death Certificate is often required.

MY FUNERAL PREFERENCES (cont.)

I have/have not executed a will. If "yes" it is dated _____ and

will be found _____.

My executor is _____

My bank is _____

My insurance policies are located _____

They are:

Policy and Company	Agent/Telephone	Value of Policy

3. Attach a listing of biographial information, family relationships, church, fraternal, vocational, club or union affiliations, etc. Also include special awards or citations. This information can be used to prepare an obituary notice. If desired, such a notice can be written out in the style preferred in advance.

Suggestions for Funeral Service

This part of the form is intended to convey suggestions only. Unless otherwise indicated, your family will assume that this is only for their information, that you have not dictated firm decisions, and that they are free to confirm or adapt your suggestions.

Unless in conflict with the legal rights of others, I desire that the preferences

of _____ shall be given
               (relationship)

consideration in connection with these service arrangements.

MY FUNERAL PREFERENCES (cont.)

My preferred clergyman: _____

Alternate, if necessary: _____

My preferred funeral director: _____

I prefer to have the ceremony held at a _____
(church, funeral home, residence or other)

I desire that final disposition shall be:

Burial in _____
(cemetary)
Where I do/do not have space.

If you do, describe: _____

Where is cemetary lot certificate? _____

Entombment _____ Where? _____

Cremation. Disposition of cremated remains:

_____

If you have chosen a formal funeral service, you may wish to state a preference below.

Do you wish to make a show of your service? ☐ *Yes*   ☐ *No*

Would you prefer a service similar to one you have previously attended for a friend? ☐ *Yes*   ☐ *No*

Do you wish a no-frills service? ☐ *Yes*   ☐ *No*

MY FUNERAL PREFERENCES (cont.)

Outline as much detail of the funeral service as you desire. Consult your lodge, clergyman, and key family members. Write "yes" or "no" after the following factors and, if you wish, make additional comments:

Open casket?

Scripture or poetry?

Music: special hymns or songs?

Eulogy or testimonial?

    By whom? _____

Military honors?* _____

Bearers? (lodge assistance?)

There are other matters you may wish to specify:

Any special clothing, jewlery, hairdresser, glasses?

_____

_____

_____

Flowers or contribution to a charitable organization?

_____

_____

* If a veteran, the Veteran's Asministration should be contacted regarding the possibility of benefits. For example, an American flag can be provided if desired, and some financial help may be available for internment and headstone.

MY FUNERAL PREFERENCES (cont.)

Do you wish a wake to be conducted by a family member?

If so, provide details: _____

_____

_____

List other suggestions: _____

_____

_____

_____

_____

_____

If you are considering donating tissue or organs from your body for medical research, you should first discuss this with your family, your doctor and your funeral director. Ordinarily, such wishes cannot be fulfilled unless preparations are made in advance. In any event, your suggestions on the kind of funeral you desire are still appropriate. A donation does not usually interfere with the body being present for services.

In subscribing to all the forgoing, I state that I have set forth these suggestions only in the spirit of helpfulness. I recognize that it is impossible for me to anticipate all the circumstances that might affect my funeral.

Date _____   _____

signature

(Copies of this form should be attached to a Will and/or Letter of Instruction and given to persons who will be available and able to act at any time. If your selection of a funeral director is definite, he or she should have a copy)

**Letter to
Social Security and
Railroad Retirement.**

Gentlemen:

Please send me any instructions or forms that I may need to complete

my application for the Social Security benefits to which I am entitled in connec-

tion with the death of my _____ , _____
　　　　　　　　　　　　　　　　　(relationship)　　　　　　　(full name)

_____ who died on _____ , _____ .
　　(S.S. #)　　　　　　　　　　　　　(day, month)　　　　(year)

Sincerely,

_____
(signature)

_____
(print full name)

_____
(address)

_____
(area code—phone number)

**Letter to
Veterans Administration.**

Gentlemen:

This is to inform you of the death of my _____,
(relationship)

_____ , _____ , who died on
(full name)   (service number)

_____ . From _____ to _____ he/she served in
(day, month, year)

the U.S. _____ . The Government life insurance policy number is
(branch)

_____ ; the VA claim number is _____ . Please
(if any)

let me know if you need any other documents or information. Also, please
advise on other benefits.

Sincerely,

_____
(signature)

_____
(print full name)

_____
(address)

_____
(area code—phone number)

**Letter to
Insurance Companies.**

Gentlemen:

I am designated as beneficiary of policy number(s) _____

on the life of my _____ , _____
                           (relationship)   (full name)

who died on _____ , _____ . Please send me the necessary
                 (day, month)   (year)

information and forms for claiming the proceeds to which I am entitled.

  Also, please check your files for any other policies the deceased may have

owned with your company.

                              Sincerely,

                        _____
                                (signature)

                        _____
                            (print full name)

                        _____
                                (address)

                        _____
                       (area code—phone number)

**Letter to
Employer.**

Gentlemen:

This is to inform you of the death of my _____ ,
(relationship)

_____ who died on _____ , _____ .
(full name)   (day, mo.)   (year)

Please send me any information relating to employee benefits to which I might

be entitled as beneficiary.

Please let me know what documents and information you will need me to

provide in settling any claims.

Sincerely,

_____
(signature)

_____
(print full name)

_____
(address)

_____
(area code—phone number)

NOTES

234

<u>NOTES</u>

NOTES

NOTES

NOTES

NOTES

NOTES

NOTES

SPECIAL ORDER FORM

Crisp Publications, Inc. publishes several books that are appropriate for retirement planning programs. These fine books may be ordered directly using the following form.

TO: CRISP PUBLICATIONS, INC.
95 FIRST STREET
LOS ALTOS, CA 94022

☐ YES, I would like to order at no risk* the following CPI books at prices shown, plus shipping and billing.**

Quantity	Title		Amount
_____	COMFORT ZONES: A PRACTICAL GUIDE FOR RETIREMENT PLANNING (Book Format) (320 pages)	$13.95	_____
_____	COMFORT ZONES: A PRACTICAL GUIDE FOR RETIREMENT PLANNING (Loose-Leaf Edition) (300 pages)	$14.95	_____
_____	COMFORT ZONES: LEADER'S GUIDE (Binder) (156 pages)	$29.95	_____
_____	INVENTORY OF RETIREMENT ACTIVITIES (16 pages — Inventory)	$ 1.95	_____
_____	THE COMPLETE & EASY GUIDE TO SOCIAL SECURITY & MEDICARE (Annual Edition) (200 pages)	$11.95	_____
_____	THE UNFINISHED BUSINESS OF LIVING: HELPING AGING PARENTS HELP THEMSELVES (250 pages)	$12.95	_____
_____	CHANGING MEMORIES INTO MEMOIRS (150 pages)	$6.95	_____
_____	PERSONAL FINANCIAL FITNESS, 2nd Edition (128 pages)	$7.95	_____
_____	FINANCIAL PLANNING WITH EMPLOYEE BENEFITS (120 pages)	$7.95	_____

Postage and handling** _____

California Tax _____

TOTAL AMOUNT _____

Ship To: _____

_____

_____

Bill To: _____

_____

_____

☐ Send Volume Purchase Discount Information

* **No Risk: If for <u>any</u> reason, I am not completely satisfied, I understand the materials may be returned within 30 days for a full refund.**

** **$1.25 for first book, $.50 for each book thereafter.**